50 ARCHITECTS
YOU SHOULD KNOW

50 ARCHITECTS
YOU SHOULD KNOW

Isabel Kuhl
Kristina Lowis
Sabine Thiel-Siling

Prestel

Munich · Berlin · London · New York

Front cover from top to bottom:
Filippo Brunelleschi, Dome of the cathedral of Santa Maria del Fiore, Florence, see page 12
Herzog & de Meuron, The Olympic Stadium, Beijing, see page 140
Ludwig Mies van der Rohe, The Farnsworth House, Illinois, see page 66
Ieoh Ming Pei, Glass pyramid, Louvre, Paris, see page 100
Frontispiece: Leon Battista Alberti, Façade of Santa Maria Novella, Florence, detail,
see page 14
Pages 10/11: Norman Foster, Wembley Stadium, London

Prestel Verlag, A member of Verlagsgruppe Random House GmbH

Prestel Verlag
Köninginstraße 9
80539 Munich
Tel. +49 (0) 89 242 908-300
Fax +49 (0) 89 242 908-335

Prestel Publishing Ltd.
4 Bloomsbury Place
London WC1A 2QA
Tel. +44 (0) 20 7323-5004
Fax +44 (0) 20 7636-8004

Prestel Publishing
900 Broadway. Suite 603
New York, N.Y. 10003
Tel. +1 (212) 995-2720
Fax +1 (212) 995-2733

www.prestel.com

The Library of Congress Control Number: 2008924897

British Library Cataloguing-in-Publication Data: a catalogue record for this book is available
from the British Library. The Deutsche Bibliothek holds a record of this publication in the
Deutsche Nationalbibliografie; detailed bibliographical data can be found under:
http://d-nb.de

Project management by Claudia Stäuble
Translated from the German by Christine Shuttleworth, London
Copy-edited by Chris Murray, Crewe
Cover and design by LIQUID, Agentur für Gestaltung, Augsburg
Layout and production by zwischenschritt, Rainald Schwarz, Munich
Picture research by Veronika Wilhelm
Origination by ReproLine Mediateam
Printed and bound by Druckerei Uhl GmbH & Co. KG, Radolfzell

Verlagsgruppe Random House FSC-DEU-0100
The FSC-certified paper Hello Fat Matt 1,1 has been
supplied by Condat, Le Lardin Saint-Lazare, France.

ISBN 978-3-7913-4043-2

CONTENTS

12 FILIPPO BRUNELLESCHI

14 LEON BATTISTA ALBERTI

16 DONATO BRAMANTE

18 MICHELANGELO

22 ANDREA PALLADIO

26 GIANLORENZO BERNINI

30 CHRISTOPHER WREN

32 BALTHASAR NEUMANN

34 NICOLAS LEDOUX

36 THOMAS JEFFERSON

38 KARL FRIEDRICH SCHINKEL

42 GOTTFRIED SEMPER

44 OTTO WAGNER

46 DANIEL BURNHAM

48 ANTONI GAUDÍ

52 LOUIS SULLIVAN

54 VICTOR HORTA

56 FRANK LLOYD WRIGHT

60 AUGUSTE PERRET

62 WALTER GROPIUS

66 LUDWIG MIES VAN DER ROHE

70 LE CORBUSIER

74 GERRIT RIETVELD

76 RICHARD NEUTRA

80 ALVAR AALTO

84 LOUIS I. KAHN

88 PHILIP JOHNSON

90 OSCAR NIEMEYER

94 EERO SAARINEN

96 KENZO TANGE

100 IEOH MING PEI

104 GÜNTER BEHNISCH

106 CESAR PELLI

108 FRANK O. GEHRY

112 ALDO ROSSI

114 RICHARD ROGERS

116 RICHARD MEIER

118 NORMAN FOSTER

122 VON GERKAN, MARG UND PARTNER

124 SOM

128 RAFAEL MONEO

130 RENZO PIANO

134 TOYO ITO

138 TADAO ANDO

142 REM KOOLHAAS

146 JEAN NOUVEL

150 DANIEL LIBESKIND

154 STEVEN HOLL

158 ZAHA HADID

162 HERZOG & DE MEURON

169 INDEX

171 PHOTO CREDITS

1353 Boccaccio writes the *Decameron*

1378 Vatican becomes papal residence

1347 Devastating plague epidemic
in Europe

1381 Venetian supremacy in the Mediterranean
following victory over Genoa

1320 1325 1330 1335 1340 1345 1350 1355 1360 1365 1370 1375 1380 1385 1390 1395 1400 1405

CA.1455 Invention of book printing, Gutenberg

1434–1464 Cosimo de' Medici rules in Florence

1469–1492 Lorenzo de Medici rules in Florence

1453 Conquest of Constantinople by the Turks

1492 Start of Columbus' voyages of discovery to America

1150–1450 GOTHIC   EARLY RENAISSANCE 1450–1500

1410   1415   1420   1425   1430   1435   1440   1445   1450   1455   1460   1465   1470   1475   1480   1485   1490   1495

FILIPPO BRUNELLESCHI

A skilled goldsmith who was also active as a painter and sculptor, Brunelleschi became one of the great architects of the early Renaissance. He could not complain of a lack of commissions—in the wealthy city-state of Florence, influential families and guilds were building an abundance of architectural works in their own honor.

Classical Antiquity and High Society

In about 1419, Brunelleschi, the son of a notary, was pleased to receive two important commissions at once. The guild of silk makers commissioned him to build a house for the foundlings of Florence. In creating the Ospedale degli Innocenti, he returned to classical elements of building, always intent on symmetry of design and harmonious proportions, from façades to interior rooms. The second commission that year came from the very highest of circles. A member of the influential Medici family, Giovanni d'Averardo, ordered a chapel for his tomb from Brunelleschi. He designed the Old Sacristy (as it was later called, to distinguish it from Michelangelo's New Sacristy) in the Florentine church of San Lorenzo as a central-plan building. On a square ground plan, a hemisphere arches over the space— the decisive forms here are the cube and square. The client was so enthusiastic about Brunelleschi's design for the Old Sacristy that he immediately entrusted to him the rebuilding of the entire church.

Wine Taverns in a Church

But not all Florentines expected great things of Brunelleschi. The wool workers' guild, for example, which was responsible for building the cathedral, seemed rather hesitant. It was a question of crowning the cathedral, the flagship of the city, with a dome. The diameter of the octagonal substructure already stood at a proud 45 meters. There was no question—for such a task, a first-class master architect had to be engaged. Several applicants believed themselves capable of it and took part in a competition. The judges were undecided. It was only after two years that they were convinced by Brunelleschi's proposal. The new project manager was not afraid of innovations: he clothed the dome in two shells, of which only the inner one is load-bearing, so that he could reduce the overall weight of the dome. Brunelleschi was also inventive with regard to the organization of the work; in order to

spare the workers in the dome the tedious and time-consuming climb up and down at midday, he had wine taverns and kitchens built under the church roof.

But the clients were skeptical about Brunelleschi's inventiveness. In 1432, when it was a question of the design of the crowning lantern of the dome, the guild preferred to hold a further competition, rather than leave this task to Brunelleschi. In the end it was his design that was executed, but he did not live to see the completion of the dome: he died in 1446. The historian Vasari reported on the funeral of the great architect in Florence cathedral, without concealing that his native land "honored him far more greatly after his death than it had done during his lifetime."

1377 Born in Florence, Italy
1401 Takes part in the competition for the design of the Baptistery Doors in Florence, which is won by Lorenzo Ghiberti
1404 Becomes a member of the guild of Florentine goldsmiths
1418 Submits plans for the competition for the design dome of Florence cathedral
1419–24 Ospedale degli Innocenti (orphanage), Florence
1420 Begins work on the cathedral dome
1420s The Old Sacristy in San Lorenzo, Florence
1430 Begins work on the Pazzi Chapel, Santa Croce, Florence
1436 Receives the contract to build the dome lantern of the cathedral
1446 Dies 16 April, in Florence

The Architect as Artist

"Remember that no other memory remains of us than the walls, which after hundreds and thousands of years still bear witness to him who was their author." The historian Giorgio Vasari cites these words of the architect Filippo Brunelleschi, who was very anxious to be regarded not as a simple craftsman, but as an artist. Architects, after all, drew on the traditions of the liberal arts, above all those of geometry and arithmetic, so there was no reason not to see them as artists. A number of the noted architects of the Renaissance fought for a revaluation of their profession, and with success: unlike that of painters and sculptors, the status of architects as artists in their own right was already recognized as early as the 15th century.

left page
above
The cathedral with its colossal dome dominates the cityscape of Florence

below left
Classical echoes: the Ospedale degli Innocenti

below right
Brunelleschi's design for the dome of the cathedral of Santa Maria del Fiore

1387 * Fra Angelico,
Italian painter, born

1419 First Defenestration of Prague

1445 * Sandro Botticelli,
Italian painter, born

1405 Zheng He starts his first voyage

1431 Joan of Arc dies

1150–1450 GOTHIC   EARLY RENAISSANC

| 1370 | 1375 | 1380 | 1385 | 1390 | 1395 | 1400 | 1405 | 1410 | 1415 | 1420 | 1425 | 1430 | 1435 | 1440 | 1445 | 1450 | 1455 |

The façade of Santa Maria Novella is
reminiscent of that of a temple

Architectural Treatises

The oldest surviving architectural treatise is that
of the Roman architect, engineer, and writer Vitruvius, *De architectura* (c. 33–14 BC). Preserved
from the Middle Ages are the writings of the
French cathedral architect and Abbot of Saint-
Denis, which deal above all with the symbolic
meaning of an ecclesiastical building. Vitruvius's
text was then taken up again in the Renaissance,
above all by the architectural theorist Leon Battista Alberti in his treatise *De re aedificatoria*, first
published in full in 1485 as *On the Art of Building in
Ten Books*. Following Alberti, many Renaissance
architects, such as Filarete, Serlio, and Palladio,
also left writings. Architects of later centuries
added their contributions, until the flow of treatises finally declined in the 19th century, when
they were often on the revival of much older
styles, only to be revived in the 20th century.

1464 Cosimo de' Medici dies

1486 Maximilian I becomes
Holy Roman Emperor

1508–1512 Beginning of work on the frescoes
in the Sistine Chapel, Michelangelo

1517 Beginning of the Reformation
(Luther's theses)

1450–1500 EARLY RENAISSANCE   HIGH RENAISSANCE 1500–1550

1460   1465   1470   1475   1480   1485   1490   1495   1500   1505   1510   1515   1520   1525   1530   1535   1540   1545

LEON BATTISTA ALBERTI

Archaeologist and painter, musician and scientist, and moreover fascinated by mathematics—to call Leon Battista Alberti multi-talented would be an understatement. Particularly since the Genoese Alberti also found time to dedicate himself to architecture, and thus definitively secure his reputation as a Renaissance "universal man."

Alberti approached architecture in a roundabout way. At first he made an intensive study of the buildings of classical antiquity, above all as they were still to be admired in Rome, and at the same time read with enthusiasm the writings of classical architects. Spurred on by their works, Alberti also wrote a treatise on architectural theory, *De re aedificatoria*. But his knowledge of classical buildings was reflected not only on paper: the palaces and churches designed by him also clearly mirror this deep admiration.

Symmetry and Proportion

Alberti's first large commission came from the Rucellai, a wealthy Florentine family of merchants; he was to design their spacious residence on the central Via della Vigna. Alberti drew up the plans and the Rossellino workshop carried out the execution. The façade of the palace alone showed the architect to be a fan of the classical style: he adorned the house with an order of columns similar to those of the Colosseum in Rome. But in doing this he did not use rounded columns, but flat wall columns know as pilasters for the vertical emphasis. At the same time, he stressed the horizontal lines by placing cornices between the stories. In this way, the façade of the mansion appears clearly structured, and the impression is achieved of symmetry and fine proportions.

The High Art of the Façade

It was not only Giovanni Rucellai who had confidence in Alberti's talents. Not far from his city mansion, the Dominican church of Santa Maria Novella was awaiting completion. The Gothic structure was already nearly finished, and even the foundation of the façade had already been begun when the clients commissioned Alberti to complete it. He therefore had to incorporate his knowledge of classical temple architecture into the existing fabric. Thus Gothic pointed arches stand under niches and portals in the

lower zone, and above them are superimposed round arches. Sweeping volutes lead from the broad substructure to the sharp gable, forms from the Gothic and Renaissance styles combine harmoniously, and everything glows in white and green stone. It was on Alberti, who remained unmarried all his life, that the choice of the ruler of Rimini fell when he planned to erect a memorial to his wife. Sigismondo Pandolfo Malatesta commissioned a tomb for himself and his family, conceived, in disregard of Christian traditions, as a pagan temple. He himself and his Isotta were to be buried there, and instead of symbols of the cross, it was decorated with the entwined letters S and I in abundance. Alberti admittedly did not concern himself with the adornment of the interior, but once again designed the façade. In the Tempio Malatestiano too the architect did not conceal his preference for classical forms: the central part of the frontage for example goes back to the closely related triumphal arch of the Roman Emperor Augustus.

1404 Born 14 February, in Genoa, Italy
FROM 1418 Studies in Bologna
1435 Publishes his treatise *Della pittura*
BEFORE 1446 Draws up design for the city palace of Florentine merchant family the Rucellai
1446 Work begins on the Tempio Malatestiano in Rimini
1452 Publishes his treatise *De re aedificatoria*
AFTER 1456 Designs the façade of Santa Maria Novella, Florence
1472 Work begins on the church of Sant'Andrea in Mantua, designed by Alberti. He dies in April, in Rome
1485 His *On the Art of Building in Ten Books* is published

The Palazzo Rucellai in Florence

MICHELANGELO, ITALIAN ARTIST AND ARCHITECT

FREDERICK III,
HOLY ROMAN EMPEROR

1405 Zheng He starts his
first voyage

1419 First Defenestration of Prague

1452 * Leonardo da Vinci, Italian artist and architect, born

CA.1455 Invention of book printing,
Gutenberg

1150–1450 GOTHIC   EARLY RENAISSANCE 1450–1500

| 1400 | 1405 | 1410 | 1415 | 1420 | 1425 | 1430 | 1435 | 1440 | 1445 | 1450 | 1455 | 1460 | 1465 | 1470 | 1475 | 1480 | 1485 |

The perfect centrally planned building:
Bramante's Tempietto

1529 Turks besiege Vienna

1555 Nostradamus' *Prophecies* are published

1492 Start of Columbus' voyages of discovery to America

1520–21 Magellan's circumnavigation of the globe

1541 Spain conquers the Mayan empire in Central America

50–1500 EARLY RENAISSANCE   HIGH RENAISSANCE 1500–1550

1500–1550 HIGH RENAISSANCE   LATE RENAISSANCE 1550–1600

1490   1495   1500   1505   1510   1515   1520   1525   1530   1535   1540   1545   1550   1555   1560   1565   1570   1575

DONATO BRAMANTE

Bramante's father had decided that his son should be a painter. Donato submitted, but met with a distinct lack of success, as recorded by the biographer Vasari: "So he determined, in order to view an important building at least once, to go to Milan and look at the cathedral."

Bramante's visit to Milan was momentous, for the young painter decided on the spot to become an architect. He began by making an intensive study of the classical buildings of Rome. His first commissions brought him back to Milan, but finally, after all, he settled in the capital. In the early 16th century Rome was a great and prestigious place to build, and above all it was the popes who brought many notable architects to the city.

Symmetry

It was on the Gianicolo, a hill on the right bank of the Tiber, Donato Bramante worked on his first architectural commission. The monastery of San Pietro in Montorio was to be enriched by a memorial building to recall the martyrdom of the Apostle Peter, which was said to have taken place there. Bramante decided in favor of a central-plan structure on a circular base—that the surrounding monastery courtyard would eventually be rectangular was something the architect could not have

guessed. Three steps, arranged in circles around the structure, lead up to the little temple, the "Tempietto." Columns surround the circular building, crowned with a dome, and there is a balustrade on the upper level. Bramante's Tempietto was regarded by the next generation as a perfect central-plan building, an architectural type that was considered the epitome of ideal beauty.

St Peter's Basilica

The Renaissance embodiment of the mania for building was undoubtedly Pope Julius II. Soon after his election in 1503 he took in hand the rebuilding of St Peter's Basilica—the old building could neither accommodate the throngs of pilgrims nor satisfy the pope's ambitious demands. Julius had big plans and Bramante was part of them: he was to build a church that would do justice to the importance of Rome as the heart of Christendom. By 1506 Bramante's plans had progressed so far that the foundation stone could be laid. Bramante designed St Peter's on the ground plan of a Greek cross, with four arms of equal length—another central-plan building, again crowned with a mighty dome.

With the basilica of St Peter, Bramante had taken on the most important project in Rome, but the pope was no ordinary client: "To be honest," Bramante once summed it up, "they give you water and words, smoke and hot air. If you ask for more, you are dismissed." His fee was a comparatively small expense; the horrendous costs of the new building, despite the lively and controversial trade in indulgences, could not be covered. When Bramante died in 1514, only the choir area had made any progress, and subsequent generations of architects largely overruled his design—today's basilica reflects Bramante's plans at most in its gigantic proportions.

CA. 1444 Born near Urbino in today's Fermignano, Italy
1476 Moves to Milan
CA. 1480 Extension to Santa Maria presso Santo Satiro, Milan, begun
1499 Moves to Rome
1500–04 Cloistered courtyard of Santa Maria della Pace, Rome
1502 Monastery of San Pietro in Montorio, Tempietto, Rome
1503 Pope Julius II commissions him to build St Peter's
1514 Dies in Rome

Ground plan for the Basilica of St Peter: a Greek cross with four arms of equal length

ANDREA MANTEGNA, ITALIAN PAINTER

POPE LEO X

1452 * Leonardo da Vinci, Italian artist
and architect, born

1472 First printed edition of Dante's
Divine Comedy

1492 Start of Columbus'
voyages of discovery
to America

1506 Foundation s
for the new
struction of
Peter's Basil
Rome, is laid

1455 Beginning of the Wars of the Roses in England

1150–1450 GOTHIC   EARLY RENAISSANCE 1450–1500

1450–1500 EARLY RENAISSANCE   HIGH RENAISSANCE 1500–15

1425   1430   1435   1440   1445   1450   1455   1460   1465   1470   1475   1480   1485   1490   1495   1500   1505   1510

1546 Peak of the Fugger's financial power,
with wealth valued at 4 million gulden

1517 Beginning of the Reformation
(Luther's theses)

1562 Huguenot Wars in France

1555 Nostradamus' *Prophecies* are published

1588 Sinking of the
Spanish Armada

1500–1550 HIGH RENAISSANCE   LATE RENAISSANCE 1550–1600

1515   1520   1525   1530   1535   1540   1545   1550   1555   1560   1565   1570   1575   1580   1585   1590   1595   1600

MICHELANGELO

By his mid-30s, Michelangelo was already used to illustrious clients lining up to secure his services for their projects. So it seems only logical that at the advanced age of 71 he was personally requested by the pope to take over the most important building project of the era, the completion of St Peter's Basilica in Rome.

Michelangelo was already widely regarded as the greatest sculptor and painter of his day when he turned to architecture. The friend of his youth, Giovanni de' Medici, now Pope Leo X, had great plans for the family buildings in his home city of Florence. From 1516, Michelangelo gave expression to these wishes. For the church of San Lorenzo he designed a façade without equal: twelve monumental columns, each one several tonnes in weight, were to adorn the marble frontage. However, only one of these survived unbroken from the quarry on the building site, and the many failures caused the building costs to soar. Michelangelo raged, the pope cancelled the contract, and promptly signed up the architect for another project. It was not the façade but a family vault that Michelangelo was now to tackle in San Lorenzo: in 1520–1534 the New Sacristy took shape (as a counterpart to Brunelleschi's Old Sacristy, see page 13). The next commission followed immediately with the next Medici Pope: Clement VII had Michelangelo plan and execute the library of the monastery of San Lorenzo. The Biblioteca Laurenziana, designed in close co-operation with the pope, became Michelangelo's most important architectural work: the most prestigious one was still to come.

An Architect Against His Will

Equally at home with all genres of art, Michelangelo was now known as simply the universal genius. It was only to him that Pope Paul III would entrust the task of bringing the work on St Peter's, which had been dragging along for decades, to a successful conclusion. Giorgio Vasari, friend and biographer of Michelangelo, noted the latter's enthusiastic reaction to the enquiry from Rome: "At last His Holiness decided, as I believe, by divine inspiration, to send for Michelangelo. Michelangelo tried to avoid the burden, saying that architecture was not his real field, and since his requests were of no avail, the Pope in the end positively ordered him to accept

the commission." Admittedly, Paul III sweetened the pill for his chosen candidate, appointing the Florentine as chief director of building in 1547 and granting him powers that no other architect was ever to be given by a client: Michelangelo alone was to decide what should be torn down and what should be added. So much freedom summoned envious rivals who were not sparing with their criticisms. One reproach was that Michelangelo was designing only a small church of St Peter, a "San Pietrino," instead of the greatest church in Christendom. Undeterred, Michelangelo reduced the size of his predecessor's model, certain that the effect of the central-plan building would only be increased as a result.

The chief architect of St Peter's was already 71 when he took over the building project, and to provide against further changes to his plans by potential successors he ordered work to begin simultaneously on all the important areas of the building. It was a strategy that largely worked.

Renaissance

The Italian art historian Giorgio Vasari coined the concept of the "rebirth," the *rinascimento*, of the arts. In his view, after the gloomy Middle Ages, painting could flourish once again. Later the term Renaissance was also applied to sculpture, architecture, philosophy and literature. Characteristics of the culture of this era include references to works of classical antiquity, a debate on perspective, and a new understanding of man as the crown of creation. The Renaissance first flourished in the wealthy Florence of the 15th century, but after the turn of the century Rome became its new center. The popes above all were great patrons of the arts, for the harmony seen in buildings, sculptures, and paintings was considered a reflection of divine order. The arts were also, importantly, a vivid expression of the Church's power and authority.

1475 Born 6 March, in Caprese near Florence, Italy
1488 Begins an apprenticeship with the painter Ghirlandaio
1489 Received at the court of Lorenzo de' Medici
1504 Completes the monumental statue of David
1505 Pope Julius II commissions him to design his tomb
1508–12 Paints the ceiling of the Sistine Chapel in the Vatican
1520–34 New Sacristy, San Lorenzo, Florence
1529 Appointed war architect of Florence
1535 Pope Paul III appoints him chief sculptor, painter, and architect to the Vatican
1547 Appointed architect of the Basilica of St Peter
1564 Dies 18 February, in Rome

Late honour: at 71, Michelangelo became chief director of building for the Basilica of St Peter

Michelangelo's most important architectural work: the Biblioteca Laurenziana

right
Perfect harmony: view of the ceiling of
the New Sacristy of San Lorenzo

ALBRECHT DÜRER, GERMAN PAINTER

1472 First printed edition of
Dante's *Divine Comedy*

1532 Spain begins the conquest
of the Inca kingdom

1526 Beginning of the Mogul
Empire in India

1555 The Peace of Augsburg
is signed

1450–1500 EARLY RENAISSANCE   HIGH RENAISSANCE 1500–1550

1500–1550 HIGH RENAISSANCE   LATE RENAISSANC

| 1470 | 1475 | 1480 | 1485 | 1490 | 1495 | 1500 | 1505 | 1510 | 1515 | 1520 | 1525 | 1530 | 1535 | 1540 | 1545 | 1550 | 1555 |

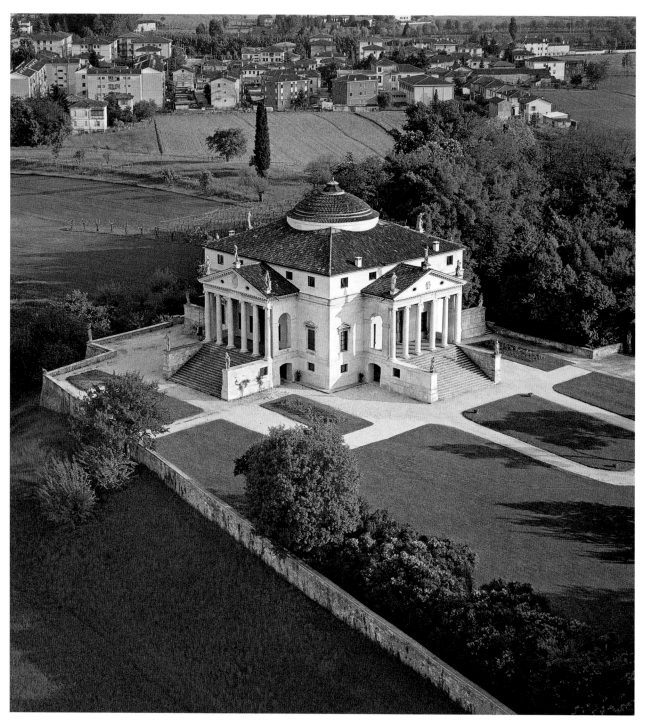

WILLIAM SHAKESPEARE,
ENGLISH POET

PETER PAUL RUBENS, FLEMISH PAINTER

1571 Benvenuto Cellini dies in Florence

1576 Rudolf II becomes
Holy Roman Emperor

1599 * Diego Velázquez,
Spanish Painter, born

1603 Miguel de Cervantes writes
Don Quixote

1618–1648 Thirty Years' War

1632 Beginning of construction
of the Taj Mahal, India

1550–1600 LATE RENAISSANCE   1600–1730 BAROQUE

1560   1565   1570   1575   1580   1585   1590   1595   1600   1605   1610   1615   1620   1625   1630   1635   1640   1645

ANDREA PALLADIO

Palladio's career reads like a rags-to-riches story: a miller's son from Padua, married, in accordance with his social status, to the daughter of a carpenter, he became one of the most sought-after architects of the wealthy. More than 60 villas, churches, and city mansions were built to his designs. And he not only immortalized himself in stone, but also left behind a series of widely influential writings.

The skilled stonemason Andrea di Pietro was in his mid-20s when the writer and aristocrat Giangiorgio Trissino recognized his talent. He bestowed the name Palladio on his protégé and traveled with him to Rome—a momentous trip for the young man. Back in the Veneto, over the next four decades Palladio followed classical principles of building—mainly for very wealthy clients, for Trissino opened many doors in high society to the young man in his lateral career move. In the 16th century, few prosperous families were without their own country villa, and their preferred architect was Andrea Palladio. His client Paolo Almerico commissioned from him a villa on a hill at the outskirts of Vicenza. A circular hall surmounted by a cupola forms the center of the building and gave it its name: the "Rotonda" is presented as a central-plan building—a daring design, for this ground plan was more usual in ecclesiastical buildings than in private houses. In the design of the entrance to the Rotonda, Palladio oriented himself to the temple frontages of classical antiquity, and gave the Rotonda no fewer than four of these. The comfort of the residents was not forgotten by the architect: he placed the utility rooms in the basement, while the *piano nobile* was reserved for celebrations, and the family lived in the mezzanine floor above.

All'antica

When Palladio finally succeeded in establishing himself in Venice, many of his villas already adorned the mainland, the Veneto. In his mid-50s, he could at last make his mark in Venice, and with the location, the building tasks also changed: the Benedictine monks of the monastery on the island of San Giorgio commissioned from him an impressive three-aisled church with a dome, whose splendid façade (admittedly probably altered by a successor) faces towards the city. On the neighboring island of the Giudecca, Palladio, then almost 70 years old, also created an imposing house of God for the Capuchins. "Il Reden-

tore," the church of the Redeemer, came into being as a memorial of the end of a plague epidemic, and this building too is adorned by a tiered, brilliantly white temple frontage. Palladio could no longer complain of a lack of variety.

His final commission too was a challenge: he was to build a theater *all'antica* (in the antique style) for the scholars of Vicenza. Once again he needed to satisfy cultured tastes, and once again he fell back on his studies of classical buildings and architectural treatises. With the help of ingenious perspective, *the architect of villas was now in addition creating the theater of the Renaissance.*

1508 Born Andrea di Pietro della Gondola, in Padua, Italy
1521 Begins an apprenticeship with the stonemason Pietro Cavazza
1524 Settles in Vicenza
1537 Villa Godi near Vicenza
1540 Given the right to call himself an architect
1542 Palazzo Thiene, Vicenza
1549 Becomes chief architect in the rebuilding of the Palazzo della Ragione, Vicenza
1554 Writes an architectural guide to Rome, *Antichità di Roma*
1565 San Giorgio Maggiore, Venice
1566 Work begins on the Villa Rotonda near Vicenza
1570 Publishes his *Four Books on Architecture*
1575 Il Redentore, Venice
1580 Dies 14 August, in Vicenza

Palladianism

Palladio's buildings and architectural writings were to remain highly influential over the centuries. In the 17th century the celebrated architect Inigo Jones imported the teachings of his Italian role model into England, and in the Netherlands, Scandinavia, and Germany many architects were also inspired by Palladio's designs. The wave of Palladianism even swept over North American shores; in the late 18th century, a number of private houses and public buildings in the United States were built on the model of his country villas. The American president Thomas Jefferson, notably, planned his countryseat, Monticello in Virginia, closely following the style of Palladio's Rotonda (see page 37).

Palladio's preoccupation with classical Roman architecture is reflected in the Villa Rotonda

Il Redentore on the Venetian island
of Giudecca

DIEGO VELÁZQUEZ, SPANISH PAINTER

FRANCESCO BORROMINI, ITALIAN ARCHITECT

1562 Huguenot Wars in France   **1588** Sinking of the
Spanish Armada

1614 Founding of New Amsterdam (New York)

1618–1648 Thirty Year's War

LATE RENAISSANCE 1550–1600   1550–1600 LATE RENAISSANCE   1600–1730 BAROQUE

1550   1555   1560   1565   1570   1575   1580   1585   1590   1595   1600   1605   1610   1615   1620   1625   1630   1635

Sant'Andrea al Quirinale – also
called the 'pearl of Baroque architecture'

1696 * Giovanni Battista Tiepolo, Italian Painter, born

1655 Start of British West Indies trade

1673 Gottfried Leibniz demonstrates a calculating machine to the Royal Society, London

1689 Peter the Great takes full control over Russia

1721 Russia becomes a major European power

1703 Beginning of construction of Buckingham Palace in London

1640 1645 1650 1655 1660 1665 1670 1675 1680 1685 1690 1695 1700 1705 1710 1715 1720 1725

GIANLORENZO BERNINI

As a seven-year-old, Gianlorenzo Bernini, born in Naples, accompanied his sculptor father to Rome and made himself useful at the latter's workplaces. His talent did not stay hidden for long: at first Bernini attracted attention as a sculptor, but soon he was in demand as an architect. And finally there was no holding him: no other artist has had such a huge influence on the cityscape of Rome as Bernini.

At the start of the 17th century, hardly a stone was still in its place in the Eternal City: streets and squares were laid out, and the Vatican was architecturally integrated into the city, for it was the popes themselves who were strenuously promoting urban modernization. And in the course of his career over more than six decades, Bernini was able to rely on the patronage of several popes. If he fell out of favor with the Vatican, there were still illustrious secular patrons to be found to make use of Bernini's services, including King Louis XIV of France. No wonder that Bernini did not hide his light under a bushel. When there was criticism of the nose in a newly completed portrait of Louis, he responded curtly: "That is how I see it."

Resurgent Rome

Bernini combined his talents as a sculptor and architect in his largest and most spectacular fountain. In the middle of the Piazza Navona in Rome, four marble river gods are enthroned on a rock, representing the parts of the earth known at that time: the Ganges and the Nile, the Danube and the Rio de la Plata form the basis of the monumental Fountain of Four Rivers, from whose center a Roman obelisk towers up. In 1656, on the opposite bank of the Tiber, and within the Vatican City, Bernini began his most important project, the redesign of St Peter's Square. From the viewpoint of the existing square, the effect of the mighty dome of the basilica was hardly to be perceived. Bernini first designed a trapezoid arrangement, and then toyed with the idea of a circular shape. Finally, he decided in favor of two adjoining areas, appropriate to the huge dimensions of the church: the Piazza Obliqua, 140 meters in depth, consists of an ellipse running diagonally to the church, to which is adjoined the Piazza Retta, which widens in trapezoid shape to 90 meters towards the basilica of St Peter. At the edges of both areas, Bernini placed wide rows of columns to enclose the Baroque complex effectively.

A tireless worker, Bernini continually pursued parallel tasks to this one, including the building of the church of Sant'Andrea on the Quirinal Hill. The decisive shape of this Jesuit church is the oval, and the ground-plan oval is even set diagonally. A circular staircase leads up to the portal, which in its turn is shielded by a canopy. Curved walls project on to the street from the portal. Bernini's urge to design did not stop at the façade: the design extends to the interior too, where the oval forms are continued. The architect himself often visited the little church even after its completion, considering it one of his masterpieces.

1598 Born 7 December, in Naples, Italy
1624–33 Baldacchino for St Peter's, Rome
1629 Becomes architect of the Masons' Lodge of St Peter's
1647–52 Cornaro Chapel in Santa Maria della Vittoria, Rome
1648–51 The Fountain of Four Rivers on the Piazza Navona
1650 Work begins on Palazzo Ludovisi, Rome
1656–67 Designs St Peter's Square, Rome
1657–66 Cathedra Petri, St Peter's
1658–61 The churches of Sant'Andrea al Quirinale, Rome, and San Tommaso da Villanova, Castel Gandolfo
1662–64 Santa Maria dell'Assunzione, Ariccia
1664 Work begins on Palazzo Chigi, Rome
1665 Travels to France at the invitation of Louis XIV
1671–78 Tomb of Pope Alexander VII, St Peter's
1680 Dies 28 November, in Rome

The Fountain of the Four Rivers on the Piazza Navona

following double page
Bernini's monumental work: the redesign of St Peter's Square

LOUIS XIV, SUN KING

REMBRANDT VAN RIJN, DUTCH PAINTER

1668 Beginning of construction of Versailles

1683 Turks bes
Vienna

1618–1648 Thirty Year's War

1676 First measurement
of the speed of light,
by Ole Rømer

1665 *Girl with a Pearl Earring,*
Jan Vermeer

BAROQUE 1600–1730

| 1600 | 1605 | 1610 | 1615 | 1620 | 1625 | 1630 | 1635 | 1640 | 1645 | 1650 | 1655 | 1660 | 1665 | 1670 | 1675 | 1680 | 1685 |

1703 Beginning of construction of Buckingham Palace

1702–1710 Last Huguenot War in France

1719 Beginning of construction of the Würz-burg Residence, Balthasar Neumann

1744 Baker's (later Sotheby's) is founded in London

1740 Frederick II (the Great) becomes King of Prussia

1755 Lisbon earthquake

1762 Catherine II (the Great) becomes Tsarina of Russia

1600–1730 BAROQUE   ROCOCO 1730–1770

1730–1770 ROCOCO   NEO-CLASSICISM

| 1690 | 1695 | 1700 | 1705 | 1710 | 1715 | 1720 | 1725 | 1730 | 1735 | 1740 | 1745 | 1750 | 1755 | 1760 | 1765 | 1770 | 1775 |

CHRISTOPHER WREN

It was a self-taught man, of all people, who was to become one of the most famous British architects. Christopher Wren's name is synonymous with London's largest church, St Paul's Cathedral, which kept its builder occupied for 35 years. At the age of 78, Wren had the great good fortune to see the completion of the building—quite an achievement, in view of its built surface area of more than 8,000 square meters.

At an early age, Christopher Wren, who grew up in a rural area of Wiltshire in the southwest of England, became enthusiastic about the sciences. After studying at Oxford, he began a professorship in London, and taught astronomy there and later in Oxford. That he was entrusted with building or restoring almost 50 churches, Wren owed not only to his talent, but also to a tragic accident. In September 1666, the Great Fire of London raged for four days and four nights. After the devastating fire, a huge program of rebuilding was speedily undertaken: 13,200 houses and 87 parish churches needed to be replaced. At this point in time, Wren had already become known with his first designs and buildings, and this was his opportunity to make his mark in the capital on a grand scale. Two years after the Great Fire, the self-taught architect was asked to draft a plan for the reconstruction of St Paul's Cathedral, for this church dedicated to the Apostle Paul had also fallen victim to the fire. Wren suggested a central-plan building, such as was known in the Italian High Renaissance, but the clients rejected the proposal as being too daring (too Catholic) for a major Protestant church. Patience was the watchword over the years that followed, and it was not until 1675 that Wren's design, meanwhile greatly modified, found acceptance.

A Versatile Master Builder

In the meantime Wren had finally decided in favor of architecture and against his post of professor of astronomy. His courage was rewarded by a plethora of commissions; in 1677 almost 30 of his designs were being executed at the same time. For St Paul's, Wren relied on two quite different traditions, for he was able to draw on Renaissance architecture as much as on Baroque. The façade with two towers and a vestibule, supported by columns and crowned by a pediment, is reminiscent of classical temple frontages as Palladio too invoked them (see page 23). In the interior, the space, arranged on a cruciform ground plan, opens upwards into a high cupola—Wren's trademark and, for a long time, a symbol of London.

Despite all the life-blood that the master builder dedicated to his grand project, other commissions received due attention. Wren remained attached to Oxford, where he had studied and later taught, as can be seen in the Sheldonian Theatre, St John's College, and Christ Church Tower. In Cambridge he designed, among other buildings, the library of Trinity College, and when he died in London at the venerable age of 91 he could also number among his buildings several palaces and hospitals he had built to royal commissions.

1632 Born 20 October, in East Knoyle, Wiltshire, England
1664–69 Sheldonian Theatre, Oxford
1665 Meets Bernini in France
1666 Great Fire of London
1676–92 Library of Trinity College, Cambridge
1673 Gives up his professorship in Oxford in favor of architecture
1675 St Paul's Cathedral, London, begun
1690 Work begins on Hampton Court Palace, London
1696–1716 Royal Hospital, Greenwich, London
1710 St Paul's Cathedral completed
1723 Dies 25 February, in London

Varied influences in harmony:
St Paul's Cathedral

1668 Beginning of construction of Versailles

1648 End of Thirty Year's War

1683 Turks besiege Vienna

1699 Austria becomes a major European power

1703 Beginning of construction of Buckingham Palace

BAROQUE 1600–1730

| 1640 | 1645 | 1650 | 1655 | 1660 | 1665 | 1670 | 1675 | 1680 | 1685 | 1690 | 1695 | 1700 | 1705 | 1710 | 1715 | 1720 | 1725 |

right
View of the church of the Vierzehnheiligen

below
Impressively magnificent building
for the Prince Bishop: the Würzburg
Residence

JOHANN WOLFGANG VON GOETHE,
GERMAN POET

1755 * Marie Antoinette,
Queen of France, born

1775–1783 American
Revolutionary War

1776 Declaration of Inde-
pendence in the USA

1791 Construction of the Brandenburg
Gate in Berlin completed

1792 France becomes a republic

1789 Start of the French Revolution

1804 Napoleon Bona-
parte becomes
French Emperor

OQUE   ROCOCO 1730–1770

1730–1770 ROCOCO   NEO-CLASSICISM 1770–1840

1730   1735   1740   1745   1750   1755   1760   1765   1770   1775   1780   1785   1790   1795   1800   1805   1810   1815

BALTHASAR NEUMANN

Whether it was a question of a new church or a magnificent palace, during the first half of the 18th century many important German clients favored only one man—the Bohemian-born Balthasar Neumann. His name was heard everywhere, his trademark being magnificent staircases.

Neumann's beginnings were comparatively modest. The son of two cloth-makers, he was apprenticed to his godfather, a metal caster. But as a 25-year-old, having meanwhile moved to Würzburg, Neumann became deeply involved in other interests. He entered the artillery, which enabled him to begin a career as an engineer, and to receive further training in hydraulics, geometry, fortifications, and architecture.

The Home of a Prince-Bishop

Neumann's talents were in demand as early as 1715, when the influential Schönborn family commissioned him to build a fountain for the family palace. They were clearly satisfied with the result, for further commissions followed immediately. The Schönborns were to become the master builder's most important patrons. When Johann Philipp Franz von Schönborn was chosen as Prince-Bishop of Würzburg in 1719, his preferred architect was already in place: under Neumann's direction, work began on the Prince-Bishop's new residence. Together with Lucas von Hildebrandt, Maximilian von Welsch and a number of other artists he created, over the next decade and a half, a superb complex, whose four wings surround a *cour d'honneur* (a courtyard for ceremonial occasions). For one of the structural high points, the impressive staircase, Neumann made himself personally responsible. From the entrance hall on the ground floor, a wide step leads to a gallery placed around the staircase. To ascend, visitors must first climb the lower flight of steps and thus reach a landing. Now they have to change direction and decide in favor of one of the two flights of stairs leading to the gallery. With this sophisticated arrangement, Neumann succeeded in directing the visitor's gaze slowly but surely upwards—above the white stucco decorations of the gallery walls, step by step there opens up a view of a monumental ceiling fresco, executed by the Venetian artist Giovanni Battista Tiepolo.

For Pilgrims and Baroque Fans

It was not only for innovative staircase designs that Neumann was engaged over the years that followed. He also found ample opportunities to prove himself in church architecture. He created a number of churches that clearly illustrate that there were no limits to his wealth of invention. In Vierzehnheiligen, a Bavarian pilgrimage church, for example, he created a ground plan composed of ovals of various sizes. The façade of the building, flanked by two towers, projects in the central area, and in the interior too Neumann stressed its three-dimensionality, so that the church appears almost to move— a feast for the eyes for both religious and architectural pilgrims.

1687 Born 27 January, in Eger, Bohemia
(today Cheb, Czech Republic)
1711 Settles in Würzburg, Germany
1715 Fountain for the palace of the
Schönborn family in Gaibach
1719–41 Würzburg Residence
1720 Work begins on the palace at
Bruchsal
1735 Staircase of the Würzburg
Residence
1741–44 Staircase in Schloss
Augustusburg, Brühl
1742–45 Church of the Trinity,
Gaibach
1745–92 Collegiate church, Neresheim
1746–51 Holy Staircase in Poppels-
dorf, Bonn
1753 Dies 19 August, in Würzburg

Baroque

The Baroque was the age of opulence, spectacle, and impressive display. With their major commissions, influential rulers, both religious and secular, determined the character of the rich creative products of 17th- and 18th-century art. The declared aim, above all in Catholic Europe, was nothing less than the creation of a "total work of art": all artistic forms of expression were meant to work together, architecture, sculpture and painting as well as literature and gardening, fashion and music. The final form of the Baroque style, lighter in style and mood, is known as Rococo.

ÉTIENNE-LOUIS BOULLÉE, FRENCH ARCHITECT

FRIEDRICH VON SCHILLER, GERMAN POET

1721 Russia becomes a major
European power

1723 Christopher Wren, English architect, dies

1755 * Marie Antoinette,
Queen of France, born

1760 England conquers Canada

1776 Declaration of
Independence in
the USA

1600–1730 BAROQUE   ROCOCO 1730–1770

1730–1770 ROCOCO   NEO-CLASSICISM 1770–1840

1700   1705   1710   1715   1720   1725   1730   1735   1740   1745   1750   1755   1760   1765   1770   1775   1780   1785

Ideal city instead of a factory: the Saline
du Roi

right page
Architectural utopia: design of the Saline

1826 First photograph

1840 * Auguste Rodin, French sculptor, born

1789 Start of the French Revolution

1848 The Communist Manifesto,
Marx/Engels

1793 The Death of Marat, Jacques-Louis David

1863 Déjeuner sur l'Herbe,
Édouard Manet

1770–1840 NEO-CLASSICISM REVIVALISM 1840–1895

1790   1795   1800   1805   1810   1815   1820   1825   1830   1835   1840   1845   1850   1855   1860   1865   1870   1875

NICOLAS LEDOUX

When a barrel maker's workshop is in the form of a barrel, or a river watchman sees a river flowing through his house, we are dealing with "speaking architecture." With his progressive social and architectural ideas, Claude-Nicolas Ledoux, who appreciated classical literature and preferred to describe himself as an architect-philosopher, was among its most imaginative representatives.

This French architect first learned his trade in Paris; his teacher, Jacques François Blondel, was a champion of Neo-Classicism. His first job, in local government, took Ledoux out of the capital.

From the Provinces to Paris
In the provinces of Burgundy and Champagne his responsibilities covered the construction of bridges, schools and transport routes, as well as farming matters and farmers' living conditions. At the same time, the young architect made the acquaintance of high administrative officials, from whose ranks many of his later commissions came. When in 1764 Ledoux married the daughter of a court musician, his connections were definitively established: exchanging his administrative work for numerous commissions from the court, he could now settle in the capital and start building for the Paris nobility. Ledoux' approach was eclectic, and he sometimes quoted from classical antiquity, at other times from the Italian Renaissance or French Neo-Classicism. In his façade for the Hôtel d'Uzès, for example, he employed the Baroque, while for the Hotel d'Halwyll he drew upon Neo-Classicism.

Ideal Town
In 1771 the 35-year-old Ledoux was engaged to build a salt works in the east of the country. Between Arc and Senans, near Besançon, he created from 1774 the Saline du Roi. Ledoux was not satisfied with a simple factory; he designed a whole ideal town for working people. Processing areas and workshops were to be grouped in a semicircle around the house of the director, and these in turn were surrounded by houses and public buildings such as churches and communal baths. Only part of his design was realized, but this already demonstrates the concept behind it: living and working were to be closely linked. Simple geometric forms such as cubes, spheres and pyramids determined the design of the buildings. The salt works began operating in 1779,

and more than 250 workers lived in Ledoux' houses. He continued to dedicate himself to his ideal city, but many of his "speaking buildings," expressing utopian ideals in Neo-Classical forms, were never executed.

With the outbreak of the French Revolution, Ledoux' public and private commissions dried up; in 1793, the former royal architect even spent a short time in prison. During his last years, he devoted himself to his writings on architectural theory, the first (and only) volume appearing two years before his death.

1736 Born 21 March, in Dormans, Champagne, France
1764 Works for the Département des Eaux et Forêts in Burgundy
1764–66 Hôtel d'Hallwyl, Paris
1769–71 The Hôtel Montmorency, Paris (demolished)
1771 Becomes commissaire du Roi
1774–79 The Royal Saline d'Arc-et-Senans
1775–83 Theater at Besançon
1776 Designs for a prison and Palace of Justice in Aix-en-Provence
1778–81 Hôtel Thélusson, Paris (demolished)
1804 Publishes the first volume of his writings, L'Architecture considérée sous le rapport de l'art, des moeurs et de la législation
1806 Dies 19 November, in Paris

NAPOLEON BONAPARTE, FRENCH EMPEROR

1775–1783 Revolutionary W

1703 Beginning of construction
of Buckingham Palace

1776 Declaration of Independence in the USA

1600–1730 BAROQUE   ROCOCO 1730–1770   1730–1770 ROCOCO   NEO-CLASSICISM 1770–1840

1700   1705   1710   1715   1720   1725   1730   1735   1740   1745   1750   1755   1760   1765   1770   1775   1780   1785

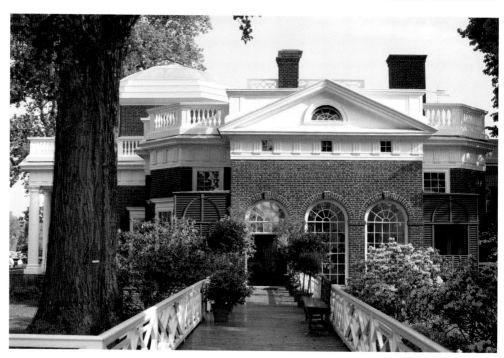

above
Modelled on Palladio: Monticello,
near Charlottesville

right
The President's country residence
houses, among other things,
Jefferson's large private library

EDGAR ALLAN POE, AMERICAN POET

1789 Start of the French Revolution

1793 Foundation stone for the new
construction of the Capitol is laid

1804 Napoleon Bonaparte becomes French Emperor

1815 * Otto von Bismarck,
German statesman, born

1826 First photograph

1840 * Auguste Rodin,
French sculptor, born

1848 *The Communist Manifesto*,
Marx/Engels

1863 *Déjeuner sur l'Herbe*,
Édouard Manet

1869 The Transcontinen-
tal Railroad is
completed in
Promontory, Utah

1770–1840 NEO-CLASSICISM   REVIVALISM 1840–1895

1790   1795   1800   1805   1810   1815   1820   1825   1830   1835   1840   1845   1850   1855   1860   1865   1870   1875

THOMAS JEFFERSON

In Virginia in the east of the newly founded United States of America, architecture largely followed European styles. It was above all the buildings of classical Rome that inspired master builders, and so both private and public buildings displayed temple façades, columned entrance halls, and elegant domes. America's third president was among these enthusiastic builders.

Classical Sources

Thomas Jefferson, lawyer, politician, and architect, built his country house Monticello around 1770 in the middle of an old tobacco plantation at the gates of the little town of Charlottesville. On this "little mountain" one could imagine oneself suddenly transplanted to a time several centuries ago.

The portal of this residence already resembles the front of a temple; mighty columns support a profiled cornice on which rests a classical pediment. At the rear, too, a similar portico leads into the building. Projecting side wings are set back from the prominent porch, and the house is crowned by a central dome. For his new building, Jefferson made use of European architectural models, such as the Roman Pantheon, but also a masterwork of Renaissance architecture, the Villa Rotonda (see page 23), which itself was based on classical buildings. This central-plan building, which had been built well over 200 years earlier near Vicenza in Italy by Andrea Palladio, was the American's chief inspiration, above all in the matter of the design of the façade.

Jefferson's Other Architectural Works

Jefferson's comfortable countryseat was only the beginning of his career as an architect. As his next project, Jefferson took on the seat of government of his home state, Virginia. In its capital, Richmond, he built the Virginia State Capitol. Anyone who had expected modern architecture for the young nation must have had quite a surprise. On a hill above the city, from 1785 a classical temple began to arise, its declared model this time being a temple from Roman times, the Maison Carrée in Nîmes, in the south of France.

Politicians gathered there for the first time after seven years of building. At the very top of the agenda for the delegates and Governor Jefferson were topics such as the abolition of feudal privileges, the separation of church and state, and the setting up of a public education system. The latter was energeti-

cally taken in hand by Jefferson himself; after his term of office as third president of the United States had come to an end, he built and financed the University of Virginia, designing a whole "academic village." For each of the ten faculties to be taught he designed a separate pavilion, which contained teaching and residential areas. In designing the library, Jefferson seems to have once again had the Pantheon in mind; an impressive dome adorns the building and provides daylight. In March 1825 the first 123 students began their studies in Virginia. Jefferson also concerned himself with their physical well being, and several of them enjoyed Sunday dinner in the ex-president's house. Among the students there were some of the finest minds of the young nation, including the founder of crime fiction, Edgar Allan Poe.

1743 Born 13 April, in Albemarle
County, Virginia
1760S Studies law
FROM 1767 Practices as a lawyer
1772 Marries Martha Wayles Skelton
1774 Serves as a delegate from Virginia
to Congress. Prepares the
Declaration of Independence for
the colonies
1779–81 Serves as Governor of Virginia
1785–89 Active as a diplomat in
France. On his return to the USA
he becomes Foreign Minister
1786 Signs a declaration on religious
freedom
1796 Becomes vice-president
1801–09 Serves as the third president
of the United States
1825 The University of Virginia opens
its doors
1826 Dies 4 July, in Monticello, Virginia

1789 Start of the French Revolution   **1826** First photogr

1776 American Declaration of Independence   **1803** * Gottfried Semper, German architect, born

1819 * Queen Victoria
Britain born

1730–1770 ROCOCO   NEO-CLASSICISM 1770–1840

| 1740 | 1745 | 1750 | 1755 | 1760 | 1765 | 1770 | 1775 | 1780 | 1785 | 1790 | 1795 | 1800 | 1805 | 1810 | 1815 | 1820 | 1825 |

Schinkel's Altes Museum in Berlin
now houses the collection of classical
antiquities

CLAUDE MONET, FRENCH PAINTER

1843 First publication of Charles
Dickens' *A Christmas Carol*

1848 *The Communist Manifesto*, Marx/Engels

1863 *Déjeuner sur l'Herbe*,
Édouard Manet

1870–1871 Franco-Prussian War

1871 Foundation of the German Empire

1873 Jules Verne's *Around the World
in 80 Days* is published

1905/07 Foundation of
Die Brücke (The Bridge)
and *Der Blaue Reiter*
(The Blue Rider) art
groups

1770–1840 NEO-CLASSICISM   REVIVALISM 1840–1895   1840–1895 REVIVALISM   1895–1910 ART NOUVEAU   MODERNISM

1830   1835   1840   1845   1850   1855   1860   1865   1870   1875   1880   1885   1890   1895   1900   1905   1910   1915

KARL FRIEDRICH SCHINKEL

One of the most prolific German architects of the first half of the 19th century, Karl Friedrich Schinkel created more than 150 buildings in Germany and Poland, most of which are still to be seen today—churches and museums, palaces and monuments, bridges, schools, theaters and castles. He was also a accomplished painter, stage set designer, and interior decorator.

1781 Born 13 March, in Neuruppin,
Germany
1794 The Schinkel family moves to
Berlin
1798 Becomes a pupil of David Gilly
1803–05 Spends time in Italy
1815 Becomes the Privy Chief Building
Advisor
1820 Appointed professor of architecture and a member of the senate
of the Academy
1817–18 Neue Wache (New Guard
House) at the Forum Fridicianum,
Berlin
1818–21 Schauspielhaus (theater) at
the Gendarmenmarkt, Berlin
1821 Church of St Nicholas, Magde-
burg-Neustadt
1822–25 Academic Museum of Art
(formerly of Anatomy), Hof-
garten, Bonn
1823–29 Old Museum, Lustgarten,
Berlin
1824–30 Friedrichswerder Church,
Berlin
1825 Work begins on the Academy of
Building (destroyed); lighthouse,
Kap Arkona, Rügen
1826–29 Schloss Charlottenhof in
Sanssouci Park, Potsdam
1830–37 Church of St Nicholas,
Potsdam
1838–65 Schloss Kamenz, Silesia
1841 Dies 9 October, in Berlin

Fitness For Purpose

His career proceeded rapidly; as early as 1815, in his mid-1930s, he was appointed chief building advisor and was given important commissions, including the construction of a guardhouse for the royal palace. After the theater in the center of Berlin, in the Gendarmenmarkt, had burnt down, the king's choice fell once again on the master builder from Brandenburg. Its replacement, built from 1818 to 1821, represents one of Schinkel's masterworks. The worthy frame-work for the new theater was already in place: the symmetrically designed square could already boast two church buildings close by, the German and the French cathedrals. The Schauspielhaus in the center of the Gendarmenmarkt welcomes visitors with its classical, well-proportioned forms, more precisely with a Greek temple frontage built according to all the rules of the textbooks. In the interior of the building, the design strictly follows the law of fitness for purpose. Schinkel made no secret of his motto:

Neo-Classicism

Since the Renaissance it has been impossible to exclude the classical buildings of Rome from the architectural canon. In the 1760s the French revolutionaries discovered Greek antiquity as a model. In the decades that followed, many architects worldwide once again followed the architectural forms of Greek and Roman antiquity. This phenomenon became known as Neo-Classicism. During the 19th century in Europe and North America, it was not only classical but also other older styles that were adopted, from Oriental building traditions to the Romanesque and, above all, the Gothic styles, a trend know as revivalism.

"In architecture everything must be true, all masking or disguising of the structure is a fault." The theater was opened with a production of Mozart's opera *The Magic Flute*. The sets were designed by the great music-lover Friedrich Schinkel.

The Old and the New

With his references to the architecture of classical antiquity, Schinkel was following a current trend. In the late 18th century, both clients and architects saw in the temples of classical Greece the epitome of perfect beauty and thus the model for contemporary architecture. Accordingly, it was Schinkel's buildings in the Neo-Classical style that met with the greatest approval, above all the Old Museum in the Lustgarten. A flight of stairs leads into the building, which, with its rotunda as a central hall, also alludes to the Roman Pantheon. But Schinkel was perfectly capable of enthusiasm for other eras. In building the Friedrichswerder church in Berlin, for example, he was alluding to medieval Gothic. Schloss Kamenz in Silesia is likewise reminiscent of a medieval castle, and other designs demonstrate Schinkel's weakness for the Romantic. Not only with regard to his building assignments, but also in respect of his models, Friedrich Schinkel shows himself to have always been open to the old—and to the new.

left
The Berlin Konzerthaus on the Gendarmenmarkt replaced an earlier theatre which had been destroyed by fire

right
Schloss Kamenz is among the many commissions executed for members of the Prussian royal family

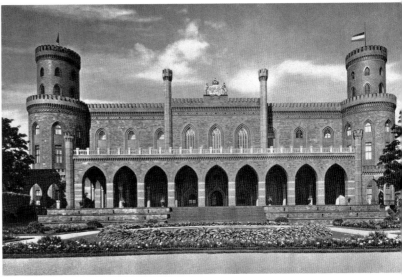

1781 * Karl Friedrich Schinkel,
German architect, born

1776 American Declaration   1789 Beginning of construction of
of Independence   the Brandenburg Gate in Berlin

1819 * Queen Victoria
of Britain born

1730–1770 ROCOCO   NEO-CLASSICISM 1770–1840

1740   1745   1750   1755   1760   1765   1770   1775   1780   1785   1790   1795   1800   1805   1810   1815   1820   1825

left
At the beginning of his career as an architect
Semper designed the Dresden Hoftheater

below
Gottfried Semper's Burgtheater in Vienna

ÉDOUARD MANET, FRENCH PAINTER

1848 *The Communist Manifesto,* Marx/Engels

1871 Foundation of the German Empire

1872 *Impression, Sunrise,* Claude Monet

1887–1889 Construction of the Eiffel Tower in Paris

1912 Wassily Kandinsky's *Concerning the Spiritual In Art* is published

1770–1840 NEO-CLASSICISM   REVIVALISM 1840–1895   1840–1895 REVIVALISM   1895–1910 ART NOUVEAU   MODERNISM

1830   1835   1840   1845   1850   1855   1860   1865   1870   1875   1880   1885   1890   1895   1900   1905   1910   1915

GOTTFRIED SEMPER

Before he decided to study mathematics, Gottfried Semper chose a career as a professional army officer.
Even when he finally attended the Munich academy of architecture, his enthusiasm for it was still muted.
Yet he was to have a profound impact on German architecture.

Born in Hamburg, Semper was initially drawn to foreign parts. In Paris he again took up the study of architecture, and this time it clearly took hold of him. In southern Europe he traveled to the classical temples and studied their coloration. Fascinated by the interplay of the arts of architecture, painting and sculpture, Semper presented his findings from Italy and Greece in book form.

Renaissance Revival on the Elbe

As soon as this project was completed, the 31-year-old was appointed to a professorship in architecture, and in 1834 he began teaching at the Dresden Academy. With his approach of linking theory and practice, Semper was striking out on new paths. At the same time, the teacher and author was given his first major project: his design for the Dresden Court Theater had been approved, and he began work in 1838. Having a semicircular form, and being integrated into the existing Baroque backdrop of buildings, the theater caused a sensation. Semper now began to receive commissions from all over Germany: his adoption of the Renaissance style had immediately found admirers.

Theory and Practice

Semper sympathized with revolutionary ideas, and so after the uprisings of 1848 had been put down he fled to Paris. Over the decades that followed, one move succeeded another; failing as a German to get a foothold in France, he moved on to London. There too he had hardly any opportunity to make his mark as an architect, and so he resumed his work as a professor. Now aged 52, in the hope of supplementing his teaching work with building commissions, he took advantage of an offer from Switzerland. He had to remain patient for a little longer, but in 1860 he was finally able to go ahead with the building of the Polytechnikum in Zurich. Further commissions, and not only from Switzerland, followed. At the same time, Semper consolidated his reputation as

an architectural theorist with his influential publication *Style*. A further success involved yet another move: Semper's designs for the Kaiserforum on the Ringstrasse in Vienna were accepted. The master builder now settled in Vienna and began work on the great building complex of museums and Burgtheater, which however was subjected to wide-ranging alterations after his death.

1803 Born 29 November, in Hamburg, Germany
1823 Begins the study of mathematics in Göttingen
FROM 1826/27 Studies architecture in Paris
1830–31 Travels to Italy and Greece
1834 Publishes *Preliminary Remarks,* and is appointed professor of architecture at the Dresden Academy
1838–41 The Hoftheater, Dresden (demolished)
1840 Synagogue, Dresden (demolished)
1847–55 Gemäldegalerie, Dresden
1848 Palais Oppenheim, Dresden (demolished)
1850 Moves to London
1855 Moves to Zurich
1858–63 The Polytechnikum, Zurich (today ETH)
1860–63 Works on his book *Style*
1862 Observatorium, Zurich
1869 Moves to Vienna
1870–78 Rebuilding of the Dresden Hoftheater (also demolished)
1874 Work begins on the Vienna Burgtheater
1879 Dies 15 May, in Rome

View of the first Dresden Hoftheater

1834 First practicable electric motor

1819 * Queen Victoria of Britain born

1848 *The Communist Manifesto*, Marx/Engels

1876 Invention of the tele

1770–1840 NEO-CLASSICISM   REVIVALISM 1840–1895

| 1800 | 1805 | 1810 | 1815 | 1820 | 1825 | 1830 | 1835 | 1840 | 1845 | 1850 | 1855 | 1860 | 1865 | 1870 | 1875 | 1880 | 1885 |

1907 *Les Demoiselles d'Avignon*, Pablo Picasso
1910 Futurist Manifesto, Italy
1887–1889 Construction of the Eiffel Tower
in Paris
1914–1918 First World War

1939–1945 Second World War
1931 Empire State Building the highest
building in the world
1940 *The Great Dictator*,
Charlie Chaplin

1950–1953 Korean War
1959 Frank Lloyd Wright's Guggenheim Museum is completed

REVIVALISM   1895–1910 ART NOUVEAU   MODERNISM 1910–1980

1890   1895   1900   1905   1910   1915   1920   1925   1930   1935   1940   1945   1950   1955   1960   1965   1970   1975

OTTO WAGNER

"Nothing that is not useful can be beautiful"—this was the motto of the Viennese-born architect Otto Wagner. His pragmatism by no means stood in the way of his imagination, however, whether it was a question of a fine town house or stations on the Vienna urban railway system, his styles ranging from Renaissance revival to avant-garde Modernism.

When Otto Wagner took up his first commissions, he was still enthusiastic about revivalism; like many of his contemporaries, he borrowed from a number of architectural traditions. His preference was for the Renaissance era, as shown in the façade of the house at 23 Schottenring, which Wagner built in 1877 on the Ringstrasse in Vienna. But he and his clients were also capable of enthusiasm for Baroque forms. A mere three decades later, he had shelved the return to earlier traditions. Now he spoke of Vienna as the "birthplace of the art of our time."

Vienna Becomes Modern

Wagner's move from revivalism to Modernism did not take place in a vacuum. Vienna had become the fourth largest city in Europe, and many buildings were under construction: the new metropolis was being given a modern face. The Ringstrasse, which was being built at this time, was edged by some 850 impressive edifices, public and private palaces. And right in the middle of Viennese Modernism, as the two decades around 1900 were known, Otto Wagner built museums, academies, parliament buildings, and public monuments. By the turn of the century, his greatest project was the design of the Vienna Stadtbahn, the urban rail network.

From 1894, Wagner, a government building advisor and professor of architecture, showed himself to be open to new ideas. For his many designs for railway stations and bridges he placed iron, always lacquered in green, in prominent positions. Curving lines and ornamentation recalling foliage show his interest in Art Nouveau. In 1899, already 60 years old, he joined the Vienna Secessionists, a group of visual artists who rejected the revival of past times.

Modern Buildings for Modern Times

Thus no trace of revivalism was to be found in the Viennese Post Office Savings Bank, one of Wagner's masterworks, built 1904–1906 in the center of Vienna. The exterior is clad in granite and marble panels, supported by aluminum bolts—a new material, like the reinforced concrete that was also used. The center of the building is the banking hall, above which is stretches a glass barrel vault. The entire interior of the Savings Bank was also designed by Wagner in the same clear and rational way. His unprecedented designs were very influential, and among the successors of this architect, urban planner, furniture designer and theorist was, not least, Adolf Loos, who ultimately maintained that all decorative ornamentation was "a crime."

1841 Born 13 July, in Penzing near
Vienna, Austria
1857–59 Studies at the Vienna Poly-
technic Institute
1860–63 Studies at the Academy of
Art, Vienna
1864 Harmonietheater and 12 residential buildings in the Harmonie-
gasse and Wasagasse, Vienna
1875 Further residential houses in
Vienna: in Hauptstrasse, Bauern-
markt, and Schönburggasse
1877 Residential building on the
Schottenring, Vienna
1882–84 Länderbank, Vienna
1894 Becomes a professor at the
Vienna Academy
1894–1900 Designs the stations on the
Vienna Stadtbahn
FROM 1898 Houses on the Wienzeile
1899 Becomes a member of the Vienna
Secession
1904–06 Post Office Savings Bank,
Vienna
1910–11 Serves as vice-rector of the
Vienna Academy of Art
1918 Dies 11 April, in Vienna

View of the Vienna Post Office Savings
Bank, one of Wagner's major works

LOUIS SULLIVAN, AMERICAN ARCHITECT

FRANK LLOYD WRIGHT, AMERICAN ARCHITECT

WILLIAM VAN ALEN, AMERICAN ARCHITECT

1826 First photograph

1819 * Queen Victoria of Britain born

1881 *Pablo Picasso, Spanish artist, born

1834 First practicable electric motor

1770–1840 NEO–CLASSICISM   REVIVALISM 1840–1895

| 1800 | 1805 | 1810 | 1815 | 1820 | 1825 | 1830 | 1835 | 1840 | 1845 | 1850 | 1855 | 1860 | 1865 | 1870 | 1875 | 1880 | 1885 |

1914–1918 First World War   1939–1945 Second World War   1963 John F. Kennedy assassination in Dallas, Texas
86 Statue of Liberty, New York   1919 Treaty of Versailles   1945 Atomic bombings of
Hiroshima and Nagasaki   1973 Watergate
scandal
1931 Empire State Building the
highest building in the world

REVIVALISM   1895–1910 ART NOUVEAU   MODERNISM 1910–1980

1890   1895   1900   1905   1910   1915   1920   1925   1930   1935   1940   1945   1950   1955   1960   1965   1970   1975

DANIEL BURNHAM

After some failed attempts at academic and political careers, Daniel Hudson Burnham started working in an architects' office in Chicago. His professional future was sealed when he met his future business partner there, John Wellborn Root. Together, they were to play a leading role in the creation of the modern skyscraper.

The two architects complemented each other wonderfully: Daniel Burnham was considered the pragmatist, while Root was esteemed for his wealth of invention. Together the pair built a significant proportion of the architecture that has become known as the "Chicago School."

Skyscrapers in Downtown Chicago

In the last quarter of the 19th century, the first sky-scrapers began to shoot up in Chicago. Above all in the Loop, the rapidly growing business district of the city, there was a shortage of building land, and only upwards was there no restriction on space. In 1889–1891, Burnham and Root added the Monadnock Building to the ever more imposing skyline. The building was 17 stories high, making it the largest office building of its time. Thick walls still formed the supporting elements of the building, but with the next project the architects were already explor-ing new techniques. In 1890 they began the Reliance

Building, whose 61 metres of height combine steel, terracotta and, above all, glass. When Root died in 1891, Charles A. Atwood took over his role on this project, and it is on his designs that the more open façade of the upper floors is based. Unlike the ground and first floor, it is decorated with ornamen-tation and designed in a more transparent way. Characteristic, above all, are the so-called "Chicago windows," which are inset into the frame structure. They consist of a large glass pane flanked by two narrow panes that can be opened.

Burnham & Company continued to celebrate their successes. Their Masonic Temple with its 22 stories was even—though only for a short time—the tallest building in the world. In 1893 Daniel Burnham became chief architect of the Chicago World's Fair.

The "Flatiron"

Burnham left his lasting mark on the cityscape not only in Chicago, but also in New York. The site on the corner of Broadway and Fifth Avenue in the heart of Manhattan seemed hardly suitable for building on: it was not only narrow in the extreme but triangular. Yet the ground plan seems to have inspired Daniel Burnham, who used the available surface area in a positively exemplary manner. The Fuller Building, which he built there in 1902, was one of New York's first high-rise buildings. The 20-stories high building is better known as the Flatiron Building, a nickname it owes to its ground-plan form, which does indeed look like that of a pressing iron. Built in the form of a metal skeleton, the building towers up to 91 metres, with the framework concealed by the terracotta façade and not recognizable from the outside. The Flatiron Building was not able to claim the title of the tallest building in the world, but even today it can easily defend its status as an architectural icon.

High-Rise Buildings
The concept of the skyscraper became established in the last third of the 19th century in Chicago. Originally called "cloudscrapers," they were build-ings whose height demanded the incorporation of elevators, a new technology. Such buildings were made possible by the use of a steel framework: it is this rather than the walls that bear the weight of the building, which can now be filled with glass. The first skyscrapers were primarily office build-ings; residential high-rise buildings were not creat-ed until the 1930s. The second great showplace of high-rise architecture was New York, where in the early 1930s the Chrysler and the Empire State Building competed for the title of tallest building in the world. Since then, this competition has become a never-ending one. At present the Burj Dubai in Dubai, which is intended to reach 700 metres high, is lying in first place.

1846 Born 4 September, in Henderson, New York
1889–91 Monadnock Building, Chicago
1890–95 Reliance Building, Chicago
1891 Masonic Temple, Chicago
1893 Becomes chief architect of the Chicago World's Fair
1895 Reliance Building, Chicago
1901–02 Designs for the District of Columbia
1902 Flatiron Building, New York
1906–09 Urban planning designs for Chicago
1912 Dies 1 June, in Heidelberg, Germany

left
The Flatiron Building in New York owes its name to its striking form

The Reliance Building in Chicago impresses the observer with its spacious glass surfaces

VINCENT VAN GOGH, DUTCH PAINTER

1826 First photograph   **1844** *Rain, Steam and Speed*, JMW Turner

1834 First practicable electric motor

1819 * Queen Victoria of Britain born   **1876** Invention of the
                                                                                                telephone

1770–1840 NEO-CLASSICISM   REVIVALISM 1840–1895

| 1800 | 1805 | 1810 | 1815 | 1820 | 1825 | 1830 | 1835 | 1840 | 1845 | 1850 | 1855 | 1860 | 1865 | 1870 | 1875 | 1880 | 1885 |

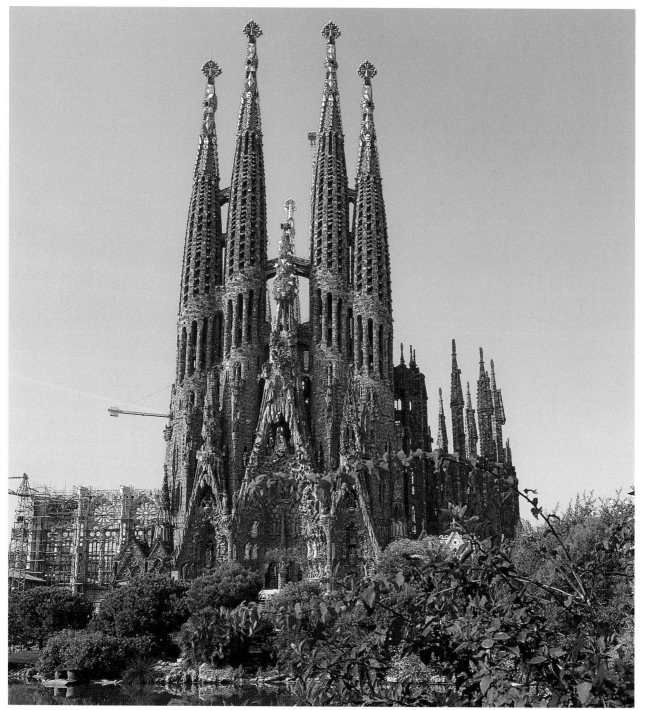

JOAN MIRÓ, SPANISH ARTIST

1921 Albert Einstein, Nobel Prize for
his quantum theory

1948 Assassination of
Mahatma Gandhi

1963 John F. Kennedy
assassination in
Dallas, Texas

1887–1889 Construction of the Eiffel
Tower in Paris

1914–1918 First World War

1939–1945 Second World War

1957 Albert Camus, Nobel Prize (Literature)

REVIVALISM   **1895–1910** ART NOUVEAU   MODERNISM 1910–1980

1890   1895   1900   1905   1910   1915   1920   1925   1930   1935   1940   1945   1950   1955   1960   1965   1970   1975

ANTONI GAUDÍ

With his rejection of straight lines and symmetrical ground plans, Antoni Gaudí opened a new chapter in the architectural history of Barcelona. With their strong colors and glittering façades, it is his highly imaginative designs that still characterize this Spanish port.

Fairytale Castles in the Heart of the City

The son of a coppersmith, Gaudí began his architectural career on a not exactly promising note: he left university with the lowest possible grade, a "pass." However, private clients above all had confidence in his skill—to such an extent that this unconventional architect was soon inundated with commissions. His sources of inspiration were unusual: he was passionate about both medieval Gothic and Moorish architecture, to which he alluded when building the Casa Vicens. This home of a brickyard owner fascinates above all by its wealth of contrasts: little turrets on the roof are reminiscent of the minarets of mosques, and patterns of colorfully glazed tiles cover the entire façade.

The young architect soon found his most important client in the industrialist Eusebi Güell, for whom he first built a palatial residence, adorning its roof with a whole forest of fantastic chimneys. But Güell had greater things in mind; he dreamt of a garden city, whose houses on a steep cliff were to offer a view of the Mediterranean. While Güell's plan did not find widespread acceptance and only two residential buildings were finally executed, Gaudí tackled his part of the work and transformed a 20-hectare area in the north of Barcelona into a walk-in sculpture. Between pine and palm trees, mosaics of glass and ceramics sparkle on the steps, benches, and houses of Park Güell.

At Home on the Building Site

"The straight line is the line of Man, the curve is the line of God"—this was Gaudí's fundamental belief. His masterwork, a church known as the Sagrada Família, was designed entirely according to this principle. When the 31-year-old took over the construction of this church, a crypt was already being built. Gaudí only briefly followed the existing Gothic forms, however. Soon he had found his model for the basic framework: nature itself. With their "branches," the pillars and supports look like trees. The Sagrada Família, as a church of atonement, was to be built exclusively from donated funds, which the master builder frequently supplied in person. Finally he realized that this task allowed him no time for further projects, and in 1914 he decided to devote himself exclusively to the church. The builders' hut became his new home. But when the architect died in 1926 after a tram accident, this "sermon in stone" was still far from completion. Of the three façades, only the eastern one had been begun, not to speak of the bell towers, the tallest of which was to grow to 170 meters. Even today, Gaudí's masterpiece primarily presents itself as a building site—although this hardly detracts from its overwhelming impact.

1852 Born 25 June, in Reus, southern
Catalonia, Spain
1878 Completes his study of architecture in Barcelona
1883–85 Villa Quijano (El Capricho) in
Comillas, Cantabria
1883–88 Casa Vicens, Barcelona
1883–1926 La Sagrada Família,
Barcelona
1886–90 Palacio Güell, Barcelona
1887–93 Archbishop's Palace, Astorga,
León
1889–90 Colegio de las Teresianas,
Barcelona
1900–14 Park Güell, Barcelona
1904–06 Casa Batlló, Barcelona
1906–10 Casa Milà (La Pedrera),
Barcelona
1910 Works by Gaudí are exhibited at
the Société Nationale de Beaux-
Arts in Paris
1914 He announces that the Sagrada
Familia is now his sole project
1926 Dies 10 June, in Barcelona

La Sagrada Família –
still uncompleted today

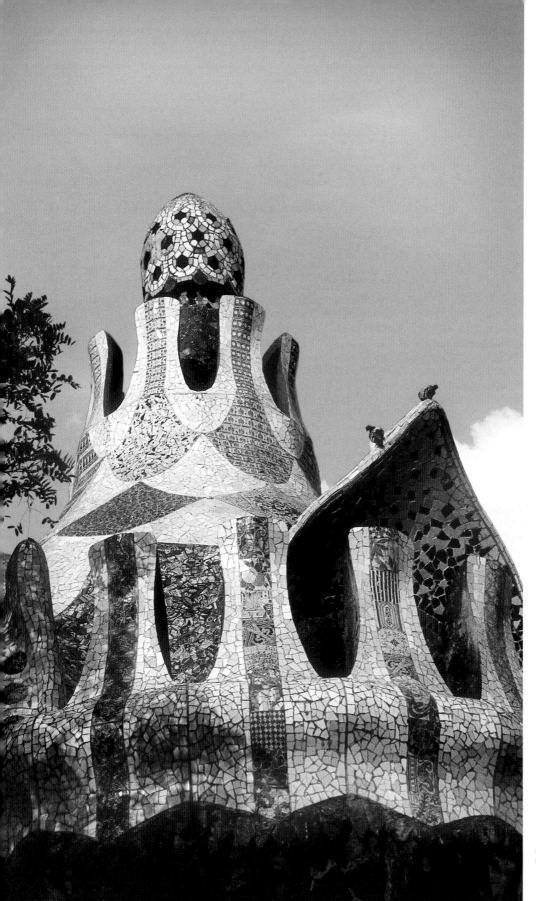

Bizarre architecture in the
Park Güell

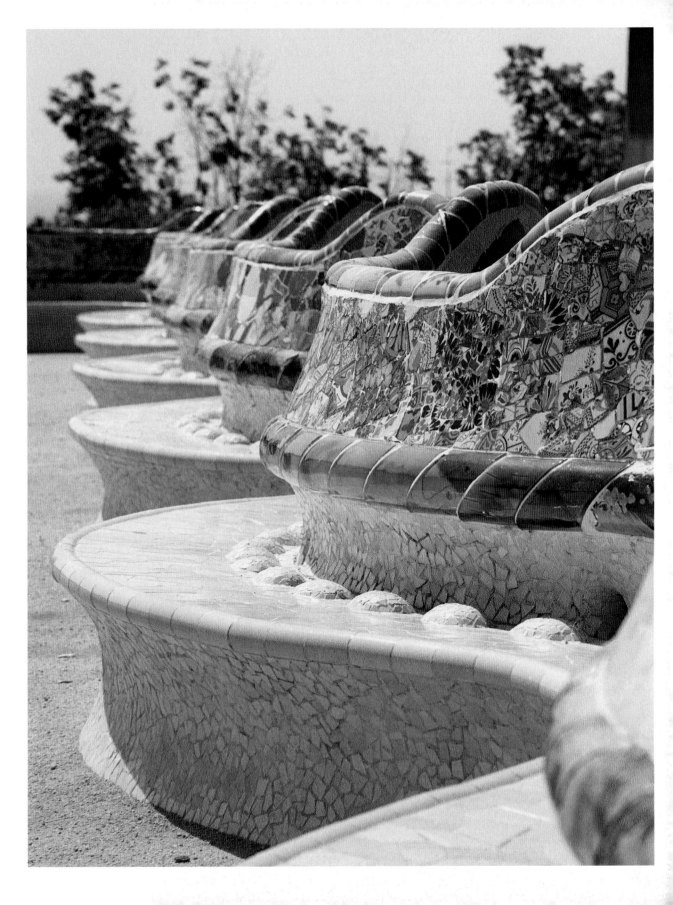

1826 First photograph

1819 * Queen Victoria of Britain born

1881 * Pablo Picasso, Spanish artist, born

1834 First practicable electric motor

1770–1840 NEO-CLASSICISM   REVIVALISM 1840–1895

1800 1805 1810 1815 1820 1825 1830 1835 1840 1845 1850 1855 1860 1865 1870 1875 1880 1885

86 Statue of Liberty, New York	1914–1918 First World War	1939–1945 Second World War	1963 John F. Kennedy assassination in Dallas, Texas
	1919 Treaty of Versailles	1945 Atomic bombings of Hiroshima and Nagasaki	
		1931 Empire State Building the highest building in the world	1973 Watergate scandal

REVIVALISM   1895–1910 ART NOUVEAU   MODERNISM 1910–1980

1890 1895 1900 1905 1910 1915 1920 1925 1930 1935 1940 1945 1950 1955 1960 1965 1970 1975

LOUIS SULLIVAN

With his plans for high-rise buildings in the Chicago of the 1890s, Louis Sullivan declared himself a revolutionary. His approach was very simple: a skyscraper, he announced, "must be tall, every inch of it tall. The force and power of altitude must be in it, the glory and pride of exaltation must be in it."

That architecture was to be his field was at first less than clear, however. Louis Sullivan twice took up an academic career. Born in Boston, he first studied in his home city, but left the Institute of Technology after only a year. Neither did he stay long at the Académie des Beaux-Arts in Paris. Back in Chicago, he was active above all as an interior decorator. But it was not to be long before, in his mid-20s, this son of a Swiss mother and an Irish dance teacher finally found his métier and his place, in the heart of Chicago.

Going Up

After great areas of the city had been destroyed by the great fire of 1871, rebuilding proceeded at top gear. For the first time, architects resorted to a new construction method: rather than building thick walls to support the weight of the building, they constructed load-bearing frameworks of steel. Over the years that followed, business and office high-rises of metal and glass shot up into the air. And

many of them were Sullivan's. From 1880 he worked in the office of the architect Dankmar Adler. The two executed their commissions for office buildings and department stores with a very clear division of labor: Adler was the engineer, Sullivan the designer. The combination worked well, and a first major commission was the building of the opera house, incorporated into a ten-story building. The trend took off, and in 1890–1891 the two architects designed their first skyscraper with a steel skeleton, the Wainwright Building. More skyscrapers followed. The Guaranty Building, built in Buffalo by Adler & Sullivan up to 1895, by no means disguised its height in the façade; the vertical is clearly emphasized in the surface of decorative terracotta.

Form Follows Function

Sullivan's conviction was that a building's structure, function, and appearance should form a harmonious whole. Architectural decoration could certainly play its part, but it should be subordinate to function. With the Schlesinger & Mayer Store (today Carson, Pirie & Scott), in 1899–1904 Sullivan provided a fine example of this principle. The two lower floors of the building show his weakness for rich ornamentation. In the tower-like extension of one corner of the building is the entrance to the store, richly decorated with wrought iron. From the third story, the situation looks different, however: the load-bearing metal framework of the building is clearly apparent, and the windows are set well back behind the steel framework. The extent of the stories as horizontal elements is as strongly emphasized as the vertical lines. This creates a cell-like structure on the surface of the building. Unlike many high-rise buildings, the Schlesinger & Mayer Store has a curved main corner above the main entrance.

1856 Born 3 September, in Boston
1873 Moves to Chicago
1879 Works with Dankmar Adler, Chicago
1881 Becomes the partner of the architect and engineer Dankmar Adler. Rothschild store, Chicago
1886–89 Auditorium Building, Chicago, with Adler
1890–91 Wainwright Building, St. Louis
1894–96 Guarantee Building, Buffalo, with Adler
1895 Adler and Sullivan go their separate ways
1899 Marries Margaret Hattabough
1899–1904 Schlesinger & Mayer Store, Chicago (now Carson, Pirie & Scott Building)
1924 Dies 14 April, in Chicago
1946 Awarded the Gold Medal of the American Institute of Architects

left page
The Carson, Pirie & Scott department store – rich ornamentation on the lower two floors

Sullivan designed the entrance to the building in wrought iron

ANTONI GAUDÍ, SPANISH ARCHITECT ▬▬▬▬▬▬▬

ALFONS MUCHA, CZECH ARTIST ▬▬▬▬▬▬▬

AUBREY BEARDSLEY, BRITISH ARTIST ▬▬▬▬▬

1819 * Queen Victoria of Britain born

1834 First practicable electric motor

1826 First photograph

1876 Invention of the teleph

1883 Beginning of co
struction of La
Sagrada Famíl
Antoní Gaudí

1770–1840 NEO-CLASSICISM REVIVALISM 1840–1895

| 1800 | 1805 | 1810 | 1815 | 1820 | 1825 | 1830 | 1835 | 1840 | 1845 | 1850 | 1855 | 1860 | 1865 | 1870 | 1875 | 1880 | 1885 |

Art Nouveau ornamentation and contours dominate Horta's house and studio

1896 The X-ray machine is exhibited for the first time

1914–1918 First World War

1931 Empire State Building the highest building in the world

1939–1945 Second World War

1961 Berlin Wall erected

1975 General Franco, Spanish dictator dies

REVIVALISM   1895–1910 ART NOUVEAU   MODERNISM 1910–1980

1890   1895   1900   1905   1910   1915   1920   1925   1930   1935   1940   1945   1950   1955   1960   1965   1970   1975

VICTOR HORTA

With his villa for the university professor Émile Tassel, the young architect Victor Horta set new standards: this house is one of the first residential buildings in Europe in the Art Nouveau style. Horta was soon in demand for his daring ideas, and in his chosen home, Brussels, Horta left behind many luxurious private houses.

Educated in Ghent, Paris, and Brussels, Victor Horta led an independent life from his mid-20s. His ideas were revolutionary. Replacing wood with iron was his first move, although it was not so much the material that was new as the place where it was used. Horta used it, for example, for the entrance hall of the house that he built for Tassel: slender iron components continue in the form of tendril-like ornamentation on floor, walls, and ceiling—and, not least, the iron columns themselves take up the vegetal motifs. Everything seems to be in movement, linked together by whirls and curves. The arrangement of rooms and passages too is determined by flowing transitions.

Building for the Workers

While Horta transposed the vocabulary of Art Nouveau with its curved lines and vegetal ornament in the Tassel house, his next major commission proved to be quite different. The newly founded Belgian Socialist Party commissioned the still quite unknown architect to design its assembly building. Horta envisaged a palace, "which would not be a palace at all, but a 'house,' in which light and air represent the luxury that was for so long denied to the miserable living quarters of the workers." The curved façade of this early major work by Horta formed a framework of slender iron elements. Brickwork played only a subsidiary role in the Maison du Peuple—the foreground was dominated by large areas of glass. The building attracted enormous attention, a situation that was to be repeated when the house was demolished in 1965 in the face of all protests.

Dynamic and Flooded with Light

Horta's later designs were no longer designed for such specific purposes, and even the target group changed. Over the years that followed, Horta created two large department stores and above all urban villas for wealthy entrepreneurs. It was precisely the latter who posed a particular problem for the architect: how could the narrow but tall town houses typical of Brussels, constricted within long rows, be made visually larger? Horta had the good fortune to have a largely free hand in realizing his ideas; thanks to glass roofs, his buildings give the impression of being flooded with light, and mirrors placed opposite each other suggest whole series of rooms.

In the urban villa executed by Horta at the turn of the century for the wealthy manufacturer Solvay, he indulged to its height his weakness for moving forms in the curved façade, whose bow fronts are vaulted. The interior receives the visitor above all with light: rooms merge into each other, walls and ceiling of the first floor are broken up into skillfully structured glass surfaces. Horta concerned himself not only with the overall structure of the building, but also with the décor and furnishings down to the smallest detail.

1861 Born 6 January, in Ghent, Belgium
FROM 1881 Studies at the Académie des Beaux-Arts, Brussels
1893 Villa Tassel
1895 Commissioned to design the headquarters of the Belgian Socialist Party (Maison du Peuple)
1895–1900 Solvay House
FROM 1897 Teaches at the Free University in Brussels
1897–1900 Villa van Eetvelde
1898–1900 Builds his own house and studio in Brussels
1903 Grand Bazar Anspach
1912–31 Teaches at the Académie des Beaux-Arts, Brussels
1947 Dies 9 September, in Brussels

Art Nouveau

Around the mid-19th century, the Arts and Crafts Movement developed in Britain: its aim was to revive artistic craftwork on the model of medieval craft traditions. Resistance to industrialization and mass production soon grew, with designers returning to earlier styles, notable those of the Middle Ages and the Renaissance.
Throughout Europe and North America, architects, painters, designers and sculptors, as well as cabinetmakers, glass artists, potters, and jewelers were reviving the traditions of past centuries. Rejecting the straight lines and strict proportions of Neo-Classicism, they employed curved lines and richly decorative ornamentation that alluded to natural and vegetal forms. This movement was known as Art Nouveau in France and elsewhere, Jugendstil in Germany, and Modernisme in Spain.

LUDWIG MIES VAN DER ROHE, GERMAN ARCHITECT

WILLIAM VAN ALEN, AMERICAN ARCHITECT

1826 First photograph

1834 First practicable electric motor

1819 * Queen Victoria of Britain born

1866 * Wassily Kandinsky,
Russian painter, born

1881 * Pablo Picasso
Spanish artist,
born

1770–1840 NEO-CLASSICISM   REVIVALISM 1840–1895

| 1800 | 1805 | 1810 | 1815 | 1820 | 1825 | 1830 | 1835 | 1840 | 1845 | 1850 | 1855 | 1860 | 1865 | 1870 | 1875 | 1880 | 1885 |

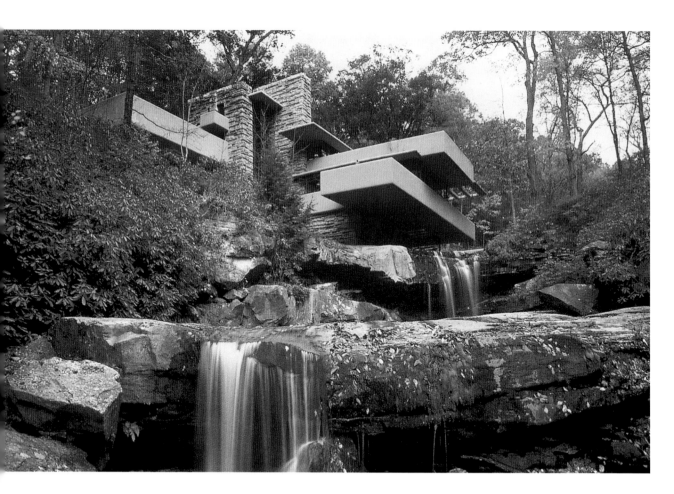

Building and nature intertwine:
Wright's Fallingwater House

86 Statue of Liberty, New York

1887–1889 Construction of the Eiffel
Tower in Paris

REVIVALISM   1895–1910 ART NOUVEAU   MODERNISM 1910–1980

1914–1918 First World War

1931 Empire State Building the
highest building in the world

1945 Atomic bombings of
Hiroshima and Nagasaki

1939–1945 Second World War

1963 John F. Kennedy assassination in Dallas, Texas

1973 Watergate scandal

1890   1895   1900   1905   1910   1915   1920   1925   1930   1935   1940   1945   1950   1955   1960   1965   1970   1975

FRANK LLOYD WRIGHT

Of his almost 92 years of life, Frank Lloyd Wright spent 72 as an architect. Unlike many of his colleagues, this devoted family man built above all houses. This self-selected focus did not, however, prevent him from designing one of the best-known museum buildings in the world: The Solomon R. Guggenheim Museum in New York.

For his plans, Wright at an early stage chose the keyword "organic." Organic architecture fits into its context—into its natural surroundings, and into its time. A new building in the 20th century, the young architect concluded, should not imitate anything old, but should reflect the present with modern materials and new technology. Wright adopted one further principle: the standard for his buildings was the human being, whose needs determined his designs. Thus the father of six children designed for his own home in Oak Park, Chicago, an enormous playroom with child-friendly low windows, wide window seats and, above all, plenty of room. Residential houses, and by no means exclusively those in the luxury bracket, remained Wright's primary task.

Harmony with Nature

For Wright, a building seemed in harmony with its surroundings when it fitted in as well as possible into its specific natural environment. His "prairie houses," for example, were designed against the background of the endless horizontals of the open prairies of the Midwest. The three-story Falling-water House takes the harmony between building and landscape to the limit: walls and floors are of wood and natural stone, while the ceilings, traversed by glass courses, allow nature to enter the interior. Seen from the outside, the waterfall that gives the house its name seems to arise from within the house itself, so perfectly does it fit into the landscape.

The Washing Machine

Wright's rejection of detail is found in the open, generously flowing room designs which he presented in 1943 to the industrialist Solomon Guggenheim, who was looking for suitable spaces in New York for his collection of abstract art. The building that finally took shape on Fifth Avenue—the Solomon R. Guggenheim Museum—in the middle of Manhattan was described by some critics as a "washing machine." But Wright was not deterred. His Guggenheim Museum looks like an ivory-colored sculpture. On the modest substructure rests a stack of round discs, whose diameters increase as we move upwards. In the interior, a spiral ramp winds along the outer wall from the ground floor up to the top story; visitors, Wright said, should first to go up the top of the building in the elevator and from there explore the artworks step by step as they move downwards. It was not just critics and fellow architects who voiced concerns: artists wondered how their works could be shown to effect on the curved walls of the building. It was clear at the opening that they had no reason for doubt. Sadly, Frank Lloyd Wright was not able to enjoy the success of his extraordinary building, dying only a few months before the completion of this architectural icon.

1867 Born 8 June, in Richland Center, Wisconsin
1887 Begins work in the architectural office of Louis Henry Sullivan and Dankmar Adler in Chicago
1893 The Winslow House Wright, his first independent commission
CA. 1900 Builds the first of his "prairie houses," in the suburbs of Chicago
1916–20 Hotel Imperial in Tokyo (demolished), with Antonin Raymond
1920S Builds private houses in California
1936–37 Falling Water House in Bear Run, Pennsylvania
1936–39 Administration building, Johnson Building in Racine, Wisconsin
1956–59 Guggenheim Museum, New York
1959 Dies 9 April, in Phoenix, Arizona

right
Exterior view of the Guggenheim
Museum along Fifth Avenue

below
The spiral ramp of the Guggenheim
Museum winds upwards to the glass
dome

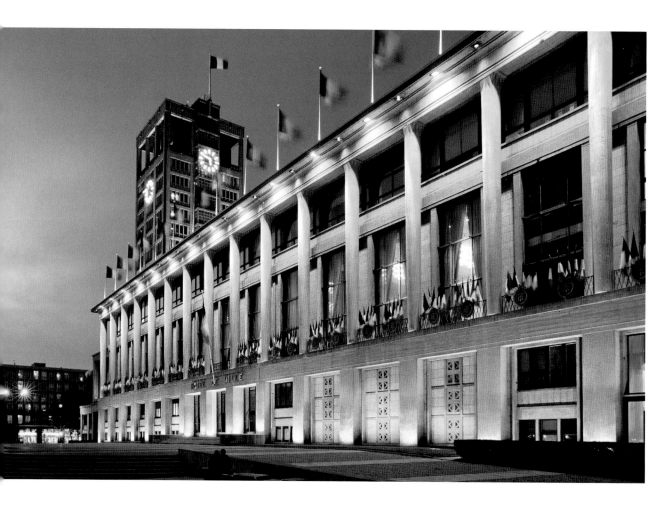

VICTOR HORTA, BELGIUM ARCHITECT

MARCEL DUCHAMP, FRENCH ARTIST

PABLO PICASSO, SPANISH ARTIST

1834 First practicable electric motor

1853 * Vincent van Gogh,
Ducht painter, born

1886 Statue of Liberty, New York

1887–1889 Construction of the Eiffel
Tower in Paris

1770–1840 NEO-CLASSICISM   REVIVALISM 1840–1895   1840–1895 REVIVALISM   1895–1910 ART NOUVEAU   MODE

| 1825 | 1830 | 1835 | 1840 | 1845 | 1850 | 1855 | 1860 | 1865 | 1870 | 1875 | 1880 | 1885 | 1890 | 1895 | 1900 | 1905 | 1910 |

The Town Hall of Le Havre, France

1956 Hungarian Revolution

1953 *In Search of Lost Time,* Marcel Proust

1973 First oil crisis

1969 Neil Armstrong is the first person to set foot on the Moon

1986 Chernobyl nuclear reactor disaster

1914–1918 First World War

1939–1945 Second World War

1910–1980 MODERNISM POST-MODERNISM FROM 1980

1915　1920　1925　1930　1935　1940　1945　1950　1955　1960　1965　1970　1975　1980　1985　1990　1995　2000

AUGUSTE PERRET

In the early 20th century, Auguste Perret discovered a still recent building material, reinforced concrete. Delighting in its clear, elementary forms, he used it in hundreds of innovative designs over the following decades.

Perret was barely 30 years old when he created a new building in the Rue Franklin in Paris, a building that soon made history. The young architect made no secret of the structure of this apartment building: the load-bearing reinforced concrete skeleton is clearly separated from the non-load-bearing filling and both are clearly visible in the façade. Thanks to the narrow supports and large window areas, the building, despite its size, does not appear at all massive, but rather light and transparent.

Perret had decided in favor of a comparatively new building material: reinforced concrete, in other words concrete cast over a framework of iron bars, which had been in use only since the mid-19th century. Perret remained loyal to the material all his life, and it is the main element of his buildings of the decades that followed. Only rarely are the façades of his concrete structures disguised with cladding, as with the Théâtre des Champs-Elysées, which is adorned with reliefs by the artist Antoine Bourdelle. This site for contemporary music on the impressive Paris street, incidentally, became talked about not only from an architectural point of view—it was there, after all, that modernism in ballet originated.

A Man of Few Words

Perret, who from 1905 worked with his brothers Gustave and Claude, moved straight on to the next commissions, his chosen material continuing to be among the tools of his trade. This is shown by some 380 executed designs. He created department stores, urban villas, cathedrals and museums in concrete—in Casablanca, Paris, and São Paulo. His work soon found its way into exhibitions and architectural journals, and Perret, who was also active as a teacher (not least among his pupils was Le Corbusier), was honored with many awards. Self-confident, dignified and elegant—this was how his colleagues described him. There was one more thing on which they all agreed: Perret was a man of few words. His eloquence was expressed in his designs.

A Celebration of Concrete

In France, though not in his much-loved Paris, but in Le Havre in Normandy, Perret made his name as a town planner. From 1945 he dedicated himself to the reconstruction of the port, which had been almost completely destroyed during the Second World War. Within ten years the new Le Havre came into being, according to the plans produced by his office, with concrete appearing everywhere, and used not just for basic utilitarian buildings. His prefabricated private houses, the church of St Joseph, and the Town Hall have a special fascination all of their own, and since 2005 have been placed on UNESCO's list of World Cultural Heritage sites.

1874 Born 12 February, in Brussels, Belgium
1891–1901 Studies at the École des Beaux-Arts, Paris
1898–99 Casino, Saint Malo< france
1902 Marries Jeanne Cordeau
1903–04 Apartment block in Rue Franklin, Paris
1908–12 Cathedral, Oran, Algeria
1910–13 Théâtre des Champs-Elysées, Paris
1912–14 Paris-Morocco department store, Casablanca, Morocco
1922 Foundation of the Groupe des Architectes Modernes
1926 Awarded the Légion d'Honneur
1929–52 Teaches at the École Spécial d'Architecture, Paris
1934–36 Mobilier National, Paris
1942–51 Place Alphonse-Fiquet, Amiens
1942–52 Teaches at the École des Beaux-Arts, Paris
1945–55 Reconstruction of Le Havre, France
1947–49 Musée des Beaux-Arts, São Paulo
1954 Dies 25 February, in Paris. His text *Une Contribution à une théorie de l'architecture* is published in book form

Reinforced concrete is used for support in this apartment building in Rue Franklin, Paris

LUDWIG MIES VAN DER ROHE, GERMAN ARCHITECT

WASSILY KANDINSKY,
RUSSIAN PAINTER

FRANK LLOYD WRIGHT, AMERICAN ARCHITECT

1871 Foundation of the German Empire

1872 *Impression, Sunrise,*
Claude Monet

1887–1889 Construction of the Eiffel Tower in Paris

1912 Wassily Kandinsky's *Concerning
the Spiritual In Art* is published

1914 Assassination of Archduke Franz Ferdinand
leads to the beginning of the First World War

1840–1895 REVIVALISM   **1895–1910 ART NOUVEAU**   **MODERNISM 1910–1980**

| 1850 | 1855 | 1860 | 1865 | 1870 | 1875 | 1880 | 1885 | 1890 | 1895 | 1900 | 1905 | 1910 | 1915 | 1920 | 1925 | 1930 | 1935 |

1949 The Federal Republic of Germany is established

1939–1945 Second World War

1960 John F. Kennedy wins the United States presidential election

1986 Chernobyl nuclear reactor disaster

2001 September 11 attacks

1910–1980 MODERNISM   POST-MODERNISM FROM 1980

1940   1945   1950   1955   1960   1965   1970   1975   1980   1985   1990   1995   2000   2005   2010   2015   2020   2025

WALTER GROPIUS

It was on industrial buildings that Gropius, born in Berlin, founded his reputation. In more than five decades of his creative career he went on to extend his field of operations considerably, and devoted himself to social housing as much as to high-rise designs. Above all, his name is linked with the Bauhaus at Dessau.

Beginnings are often difficult, and this was certainly true of Walter Gropius: "I am not capable of drawing a straight line," he wrote to his mother when he was a student. But his lack of talent as a draughtsman could not hold him back for long: after completing his studies and after only a few years working with Peter Behrens, Gropius, still aged only 20, received his first major commission: to build a factory. From 1911 he worked on this project, the Fagus factory, with Adolf Meyer in the small town of Alfeld an der Leine in Lower Saxony. The modern materials of glass and metal determined the image of the building, which is reduced to a compact and at the same time transparent cube: only in places are the glass surfaces broken up by areas of wall. In the corners, the two architects rejected the addition of supports, increasing the light and fragile impression created by the building, which also does without pediments. The only decoration of the flat-roofed building are the vertical and horizontal lines with which the façade is uniformly covered.

Not a Matter of Luxury

With this factory building, Gropius had created a masterpiece. He continued to work in the same plain and unpretentious style, his cubical structures determined by clear, white surfaces and severely symmetrical rows of windows. For Gropius, a priority was "that artistic design should not be a matter of luxury, but must be the business of life itself." Thus many of his designs even for social housing seem severe. Economically priced building meant for Gropius the use of standardized and prefabricated components, put together on the principle of the construction kit. That such mass production did not necessarily meet the taste of the masses was shown by the criticism of his residential high-rise houses and workers' settlements, including Gropius City, designed by him in Berlin.

Looking to the Future

It is above all the Bauhaus with which his name is linked. Walter Gropius was a co-founder and first director of the school of arts and crafts in Weimar, which opened its doors in 1919. Artists, craftworkers and later also architects worked hand in hand there. When the Bauhaus moved to Dessau, Gropius planned the new school building, or rather "the new building of the future." In 1925–1926, three L-shaped wings took shape, linked to each other. The right one accommodated the workshop; on the mainly glazed façade of the four-story building is displayed in large lettering the Bauhaus logo. Wide window areas also characterize the connecting area. The students' block, however, corresponding to the individuality within, is designed with balconies and single windows. After the completion of the students' block, Gropius tackled the living quarters of the Bauhaus teachers, and a whole settlement took shape. Under the Nazi regime, the Bauhaus was violently criticized and finally closed down. In 1937 its creator emigrated to England and in 1937 moved on to Cambridge, Massachusetts, where he taught architecture at Harvard University.

1883 Born 18 May, in Berlin, Germany
1903–07 Studies at the colleges of technology in Munich and Berlin
1907–10 Works as an assistant to Peter Behrens in Berlin
1910 Becomes an independent architect
1911–13 Fagus shoe-last factory, Alfeld an der Leine, Germany, with Adolf Meyer
1919 Appointed to the College of Visual Arts in Weimar, renamed the Bauhaus
1928 Gives up his post of director of the Bauhaus; opens his own office in Berlin
1919–30 Siemensstadt, Berlin
1934 Emigrates to England
1937 Appointed to teach architecture at Harvard University
1958–63 Pan American Building, New York
1965 Rosenthal porcelain factory, Selb, Germany
1969 Dies 5 July, in Boston, USA

A staircase in the Bauhaus at Dessau

left
The Bauhaus, Dessau, severely
functional

Sober and unpretentious: the Fagus
factory in Alfeld

FRANK LLOYD WRIGHT, AMERICAN ARCHITECT ═══════════════════════

LE CORBUSIER, SWISS ARCHITECT ═══════════════════════

PHILIP JOHNSON, AMERICAN ARCHITECT ═══════════════

1866 * Wassily Kandinsky, Russian artist, born   **1881** * Pablo Picasso,   **1914** Assassination of Archduke Franz Ferdi-
     Spanish artist, born   nand, heir to the Austro-Hungarian throne,
1872 *Impression, Sunrise,*   leads to beginning of First World War
     Claude Monet

1871 Foundation of the German Empire   **1914–1918** First World War   **1929** Start of the Gre
                                Depression

1840–1895 REVIVALISM   1895–1910 ART NOUVEAU   MODERNISM 1910–1980

| 1850 | 1855 | 1860 | 1865 | 1870 | 1875 | 1880 | 1885 | 1890 | 1895 | 1900 | 1905 | 1910 | 1915 | 1920 | 1925 | 1930 | 1935 |

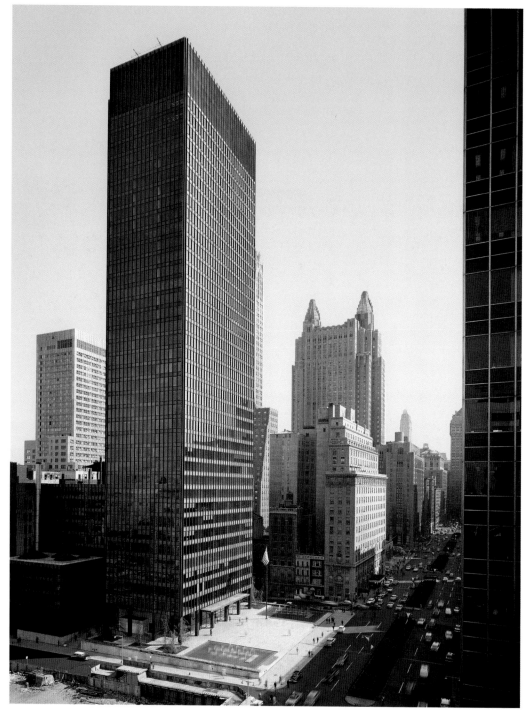

Symbol of modern
architecture: the Seagram
Building in New York

Adolf Hitler becomes Führer
and Chancellor of the Reich

1950 India forms a republic

1939–1945 Second World War

1961 Berlin Wall erected

1986 Chernobyl nuclear
reactor disaster

2001 September 11 attacks

1946 First meeting of the United Nations

1910–1980 MODERNISM   POST-MODERNISM FROM 1980

1940   1945   1950   1955   1960   1965   1970   1975   1980   1985   1990   1995   2000   2005   2010   2015   2020   2025

LUDWIG MIES VAN DER ROHE

One of the most influential architects of the 20th century, Ludwig Mies van der Rohe rejected an academic education. He learnt his craft in the office of Peter Behrens—one of his fellow-students there being Le Corbusier.

Office buildings and exhibition pavilions, factories and museums, private houses and libraries ... in the six decades of his career, Mies van der Rohe continually discovered new challenges, whether in Berlin, Chicago, New York or Stuttgart.

"Jerusalem" in Stuttgart

True to his motto that "only today can be given form," in 1927 he took over the artistic direction of the Weissenhof Settlement in Stuttgart. Nothing less was presented there than the future of building, on the occasion of the exhibition *Die Wohnung*. The principles Mies van der Rohe and 16 other architects had adopted were made clear by this "model settlement": the 21 houses, containing 63 apartments under flat roofs, were bare of decoration. The enthusiasm of public and press was muted, and even their fellow architects were critical: "In multifarious horizontal terraces, uninhabitably crowded together, a heaping of low-lying cubes throngs up a hillside, reminiscent rather of a suburb of Jerusalem than of apartments for Stuttgart ... an Arab village."

Pure Architecture

In 1929 he created for the Spanish port of Barcelona an exhibition pavilion that demonstrated his continuing development of Bauhaus architecture. Here architecture has been reduced to absolute basics: a few plain walls and a large, flat roof. The freestanding steel pillars and the stone walls are mirrored in two pools of water, while interior and

exterior space are linked rather than separated by large areas of glass.

Rectangular forms, flat roofs, transparency—the architect continued to be true to his clear, rationalistic building concepts. In 1938 he emigrated to the United States. There, together with Herbert Greenwald, he created large residential high-rise complexes, such as the apartment houses on Lake Shore Drive in Chicago. Reduced to a structural skeleton, these buildings are pure steel constructions, with extensively glazed façades. As early as 1923 the Berlin-born Mies had clarified his views on modern office architecture: "The materials are concrete, iron, glass. Reinforced concrete buildings are skeleton buildings by their nature. Neither pastry nor armored tanks." The Seagram Building, completed in 1958 on New York's Park Avenue, the architect's first office high-rise, also speaks volumes in this respect. Mies van der Rohe's office towers at the same time fit harmoniously into the urban space that surrounds them—the glass fronts of the lower stories merge seamlessly into the squares around them.

1886 Born 27 March, in Aachen, Germany
1913 Opens his own office in Steglitz, Germany
1926 Becomes vice-president of the Deutscher Werkbund
1927 Weissenhof Settlement, Stuttgart
1929 German Pavilion at the Barcelona World's Fair (demolished and reconstructed in 1986)
1930–33 Serves as director of the Bauhaus
1938 Emigrates to the USA. Becomes director of the later Illinois Institute of Technology, Chicago
1942–57 Teaches at the Illinois Institute of Technology, Chicago
1944 Becomes an American citizen
1948–51 Residential high-rise at 860–880 Lake Shore Drive, Chicago
1954–58 Seagram Building, New York
1962–68 New National Gallery, Berlin
1966–69 IBM Building, Chicago
1969 Dies 17 August, in Chicago

Transparent and light – the Farnsworth House in Illinois

A style-forming building:
the Barcelona Pavilion

ALVAR AALTO, FINISH ARCHITECT AND DESIGNER

JAMES STIRLING, BRITISH ARCHITECT

MAX ERNST, GERMAN PAINTER

1872 *Impression, Sunrise,* Claude Monet

1887–1889 Construction of the Eiffel Tower in Paris

1914–1918 First World War

1919 Treaty of Versailles

1929 Start of the Gre Depression

1840–1895 REVIVALISM   **1895–1910 ART NOUVEAU**   **MODERNISM 1910–1980**

| 1850 | 1855 | 1860 | 1865 | 1870 | 1875 | 1880 | 1885 | 1890 | 1895 | 1900 | 1905 | 1910 | 1915 | 1920 | 1925 | 1930 | 1935 |

Notre Dame du Haut, pilgrimage church and architectural icon

1939–1945 Second World War

1946 First meeting of the
United Nations

1961 Berlin Wall erected

1963 John F. Kennedy assassination
in Dallas, Texas

1993 The Maastricht Treaty takes effect,
formally establishing the European Union

1986 Chernobyl nuclear
reactor disaster

2001 September 11 attacks

1910–1980 MODERNISM   POST-MODERNISM FROM 1980

1940   1945   1950   1955   1960   1965   1970   1975   1980   1985   1990   1995   2000   2005   2010   2015   2020   2025

LE CORBUSIER

He wrote more than 30 books on art and architecture, painted and drew, and devoted himself to poetry and furniture making. But it was thanks to his buildings that he became famous: the Swiss-born architect made his name in three continents during the six decades of his active career, mainly with buildings in concrete.

Domino Construction

Charles-Édouard Jeanneret, son of a pianist and a mountaineer, began his career as an architect early in life. In his early 20s he worked in the office of the architect Auguste Perret (see p. 61) in Paris, and two years later he was active as a draughtsman in the studio of Peter Behrens. In 1914 the young architect and urban planner entered the field of the serial production of houses, developing over the decades a rationalized method of building that he employed in the design of his new home in Paris. From 1920, Jeanneret started calling himself Le Corbusier.
He made a start with the "Domino" system, based on a standardized framework of reinforced concrete, to which the client in question could add walls, windows or doors from an architectural catalogue. In line with Citroën's mechanized car production, the Swiss architect then worked on the "Citrohan" house. He made no secret of his enthusiasm for new technologies and media.

Machines for Living …

But his ideas on the city of the future did not meet with unalloyed approval. Le Corbusier's rejection of traditional city planning also found its impassioned critics—a glance at his "machine for living" in Marseille will show why. From 1945, in the south of the French Mediterranean city, he created the Unité de l'Habitation, a high-rise complex that consists not only of apartments but also shops and offices. Almost the whole urban infrastructure is present there, for it was intended that its residents need never leave their self-contained concrete "village." And it was not only his urban planning designs demonstrate Le Corbusier's enthusiasm for concrete as a building material.

… and "Concrete Piles"

It was as a "concrete pile" that his project on a high plateau above the village of Ronchamp became known. In 1950, in this hilly district some 20 kilometers from Belfort, the architect began to build a pilgrimage chapel, which was to replace the previous, destroyed structure. Notre-Dame-du-Haut was to offer space for about 200 believers, but also be able to receive the swarms of pilgrims who streamed to this site twice a year. To them, Le Corbusier offered space with an exterior choir in front of the east wall, sheltered by the widely projecting brown roof. The problem of space was thus solved in the best possible way. So is everything else right angles and straight sides, arranged in neat symmetrical order? Not quite, or at any rate not only: a windowless tower and an arched white wall, on which rests a bulging, heavy roof, determine our first impression of the chapel. Only on the north wall do right angles dominate, while the west wall is rounded off. Various large openings are distributed as though at random over the façade that frames the main entrance. Partly covered with plaster, partly exposing the concrete beneath, this design by Le Corbusier also inspired critics to invent various nicknames, but the "sacred garage" nevertheless ended up as a milestone of modern architecture.

1887 Born Charles-Édouard Jeanneret, 6 October, in La-Chaux-de-Fonds, Switzerland
1908–09 Works with the Perret brothers in Paris
1910 Works with Peter Behrens in Berlin
1925 Pavillon de l'Esprit Nouveau at the Paris Exhibition
1927 Citrohan House, Stuttgart
1930 Marries Yvonne Gallis
1947–52 Unité d'Habitation housing estate in Marseille
1951–56 Chandigarh in North India
1953–61 Extension of the monastery of La Tourette at Eveux-sur-Arbresle near Lyon
1963 Carpenter Art Center, Harvard, USA
1965 Dies 27 August, at Cap-Martin near Nice

Design of 1951 for Notre Dame du Haut

Unité d'Habitation: residential utopia
in Marseille

The church of Saint-Pierre in Firminy was not completed until after the architect's death

LE CORBUSIER, SWISS ARCHITECT

1907 *Les Demoiselles d'Avignon*, Pablo Picasso
1887–1889 Construction of the   **1914–1918** First World War
Eiffel Tower in Paris   **1919** The Bauhaus is founded

1840–1895 REVIVALISM   1895–1910 ART NOUVEAU   MODERNISM 1910–1980

| 1850 | 1855 | 1860 | 1865 | 1870 | 1875 | 1880 | 1885 | 1890 | 1895 | 1900 | 1905 | 1910 | 1915 | 1920 | 1925 | 1930 | 1935 |

De Stijl

The painter Theo van Doesburg created the Dutch visual arts magazine *De Stijl* in 1917, and it continued to appear until 1932. It was around this magazine that a celebrated group of artists and designers formed. As well as van Doesburg, Piet Mondrian was a member from the beginning, and many other painters, architects, and sculptors came together in *De Stijl*. Whatever their métier, they demanded an art that went beyond the imitation of nature: turning against the depiction of natural forms, they resorted to simple geometrical forms and clarity of color. Their works were largely characterized by horizontal and vertical elements, by the colors red, blue and yellow, and by the neutral tones black, white and gray. The movement influenced architecture mainly through Rietveld's Schröder House.

above
UNESCO World Cultural Heritage Site
since 2000: the Rietveld-Schröder House

below
View of the interior of the Rietveld-
Schröder House

1973 First oil crisis

1993 The Maastricht Treaty takes effect,
formally establishing the European Union

1961 Berlin Wall erected

1946 First meeting of the
United Nations

1963 John F. Kennedy assassination in Dallas, Texas

1986 Chernobyl nuclear
reactor disaster

2001 September 11 attacks

1939–1945 Second World War

1990 Final year of the Cold War era

1910–1980 MODERNISM   POST-MODERNISM FROM 1980

1940   1945   1950   1955   1960   1965   1970   1975   1980   1985   1990   1995   2000   2005   2010   2015   2020   2025

GERRIT RIETVELD

The Dutch architect and designer Gerrit Rietveld began his career early: as a twelve year old he entered his father's furniture workshop. At first his interest was in the applied arts, but it was not long before he was also fascinated by architecture.

Form and Color

To begin with, he seems to have been influenced by painting. In 1918 he designed an armchair made from wooden slats, whose reduced forms are reminiscent of the paintings of abstract artists. But in addition to this, in the years that followed color took on ever greater importance in his furniture designs. Red, yellow and blue contrast with black, white and gray: in this way Rietveld's armchair developed into the "Red-Blue Chair," which brought international recognition to the designer from Utrecht. The reduced palette incidentally corresponded to the colors that were used by the painters of the group De Stijl. It was from this group too, with whose members he was in touch from 1919, that Rietveld was to adopt his asymmetrical designs. This is seen, for example, in his Berlin Chair, which looks more like a sculpture than a piece of furniture. Rietveld also became prominent as a typographer, and he designed many printed items both on his own

account and for others. In the late 1920s and above all the 1930s he developed furniture for mass production and as an architect also resorted to prefabricated building parts. For his "kernwoningen" (housing modules) in Utrecht and Vienna he relied on mass production for all the essential components.

A House for the Schröders

While little is still preserved of his later residential building projects, his main work long ago became an architectural icon. In 1924 Truus Schröder-Schräder commissioned Rietveld, until then hardly known as an architect, to build a private house for her. His 35-year-old client was looking for a new home for herself and her three children after the death of her husband. When she could not find a suitable property to rent, Rietveld finally tendered successfully for a new building at the edge of the city of Utrecht. Following Schröder's ideas, Rietveld designed a small but revolutionary house. His client wanted to see walls only where they were indispensable; what was important to her was the view of the landscape and the practicality of the whole design. Rietveld met her wishes with movable walls on the first floor, which offered the flexibility requested by his demanding client. Other areas, such as the kitchen and a den on the ground floor, were separated from the living quarters. On the grounds of cost, Rietveld refrained from executing the whole structure in concrete as originally planned, but used this material only for the foundations and balconies. A skylight and generously cut windows allow light into the house, whose façades are structured by further horizontal and vertical elements.

1888 Born 24 June, in Utrecht, Holland
1904–08 Attends drawing classes in Utrecht
1917 Works independently as a furniture designer
1922 Interior decoration and furniture for the waiting room of a medical practice
1923 Takes part in an exhibition in Paris, *Les Architectes du groupe de Stijl*, Galerie de l'Effort Moderne
1924 Commissioned to design the Schröder House, Utrecht
1922–1924 Apartment blocks in Utrecht and Vienna
1931 Klep House, Breda
1936 Mees House, The Hague
1956 De Ploeg textile factory, Utrecht
1963 Design for the Rijksmuseum Vincent van Gogh, Amsterdam
1964 Dies 25 June, in Utrecht
1987 Schröder House opened to the public

An essential feature in every design collection: Rietveld's Red-Blue Chair

ADOLF LOOS,
AUSTRIAN ARCHITECT

ALVAR AALTO, FINISH ARCHITECT AND DESIGNER

1914–1918 First World War

1907 *Les Demoiselles d'Avignon,*
Pablo Picasso

1929 Start ot the Grea
Depression

1887–1889 Construction of the
Eiffel Tower in Paris

1919 The Bauhaus is founded

1840–1895 REVIVALISM   **1895–1910 ART NOUVEAU**   **MODERNISM 1910–1980**

1850 1855 1860 1865 1870 1875 1880 1885 1890 1895 1900 1905 1910 1915 1920 1925 1930 1935

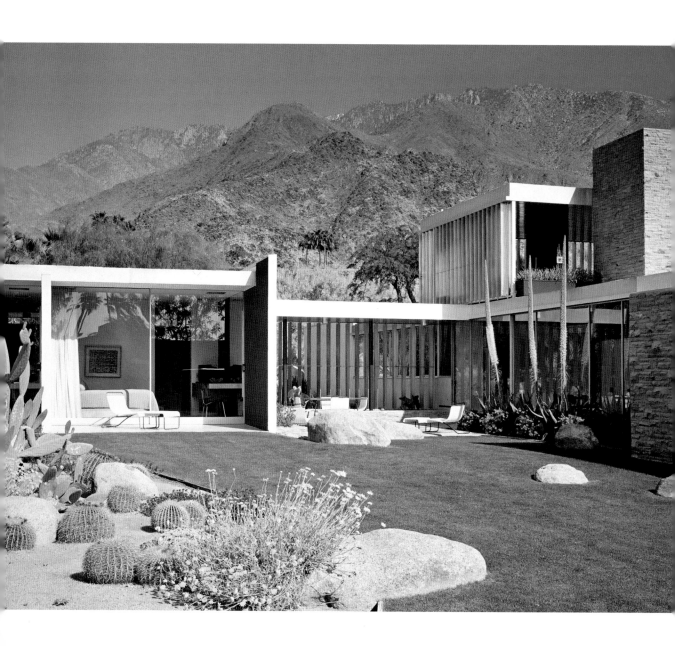

1979 The Soviet Union invades Afghanistan   **2001** September 11 attacks

1969 Neil Armstrong is the first person
to set foot on the Moon

1993 The Maastricht Treaty takes effect,
formally establishing the European Union

3 Adolf Hitler becomes Führer
and Chancellor of the Reich

1961 Berlin Wall erected   **1973** First oil crisis   **1986** Chernobyl nuclear reactor disaster

1939–1945 Second World War

1910–1980 MODERNISM   POST-MODERNISM FROM 1980

| 1940 | 1945 | 1950 | 1955 | 1960 | 1965 | 1970 | 1975 | 1980 | 1985 | 1990 | 1995 | 2000 | 2005 | 2010 | 2015 | 2020 | 2025 |

RICHARD NEUTRA

The impact of the Viennese-born Richard Neutra can be seen above all in southern California. His many private houses and villas from Los Angeles to Palm Springs are designed on a grand scale and yet at the same time are impressively integrated in their natural and built environment.

During his studies in architecture at the Technische Hochschule in Vienna, Neutra was strongly influenced by the work of the architect Adolf Loos, known for his very functional designs. But even after the end of his studies, Europe could not hold him for long: in 1923 Neutra emigrated to the USA, where he began work as a draughtsman in a New York architect's office. A year later, his wife Dione followed him, and the young couple finally moved on to Los Angeles. There Neutra worked for, among others, Frank Lloyd Wright, whose buildings fascinated the young Austrian.

The "Health House" and California
In 1927 Neutra received his first major commission: a couple named Lovell entrusted the young architect with the building of a residence in the hills of Los Angeles. Neutra built a steel framework that gave an impression of lightness—until then, these were reserved for high-rise buildings—and incorporated glass surfaces into it. From the street entrance a wide staircase leads down to the living room and finally to the swimming pool in the basement. The building was nicknamed the "Health House," not however because of its inclusion of a swimming pool, but because of its health-conscious residents. Now Neutra, barely 40, who had recently become an American citizen, raised the tempo. Over the next four decades, he created private houses at an impressive speed in his chosen home of California, supported from the 1950s by his middle son, Dion. He devoted himself to building not only villas, but also to school buildings, churches, museums, and business premises. At the same time, he was awarded honorary doctorates and exhibitions of his work in quick succession; once having passed the age of 50, he was inundated with architectural prizes and medals.

Like an Aircraft in the Desert
One of his best-known buildings is the holiday home begun in 1946 for Edgar J. Kaufmann. This client was already the owner of the spectacular Fallingwater House, which Frank Lloyd Wright had built a decade earlier (see page 57). But for his home on the east coast, near Palm Springs in California, Kaufmann had other plans. There, on a modest site of 300 square meters (and for $348,000) he created his "desert house." Neutra was inspired by the southern Californian "moon landscape": four shallow wings of the house extend into the landscape, and the walls consist mainly of glass, so that interior and exterior space merge into each other (an echo of Wright's designs). Sometimes Neutra's design is compared to a silver aircraft that has just landed on a green lawn—although the Kaufmann House, thanks to its stress on the horizontal, blends harmoniously into the barren desert landscape.

1892 Born 8 April, in Vienna, Austria
1911–15, 1917–18 Studies architecture in Vienna
1922 Marries Dione Niedermann
1923 Emigrates to New York
1925 Moves to Los Angeles
1925–50 Diatom Series
1927 Neutra and Schindler present their design for the League of Nations, Geneva
1927–29 Lovell House, Los Angeles
1930 World trip
1933 Koblick House, Atherton, California, Universal-International Building, Hollywood
1935 Corona School, Bell, California
1946–47 Kaufmann Desert House near Palm Springs
1970 Dies 10 April, in Wuppertal, Germany

Architectural classic in a solitary landscape: the Kaufmann Desert House

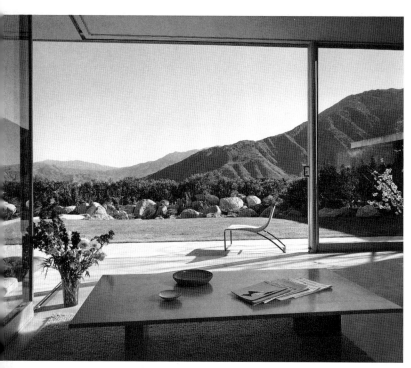

Interior and exterior spaces merge:
the desert house of Edgar J. Kaufmann

LE CORBUSIER, SWISS ARCHITECT

EERO SAARINEN, FINISH ARCHITECT

1912 Wassily Kandinsky's *Concerning the Spiritual In Art* is published

1887–1889 Construction of the Eiffel Tower in Paris

1907 *Les Demoiselles d'Avignon,* Pablo Picasso

1924 Summer Olympics openin ceremonies held in Paris

1914–1918 First World war

1928 * Andy Warhol, American artist

1840–1895 REVIVALISM   **1895–1910 ART NOUVEAU**   **MODERNISM 1910–1980**

| 1850 | 1855 | 1860 | 1865 | 1870 | 1875 | 1880 | 1885 | 1890 | 1895 | 1900 | 1905 | 1910 | 1915 | 1920 | 1925 | 1930 | 1935 |

left
Red bricks characterize the façade of the Technical University of Helsinki

below
The theater at Essen was completed to the designs of Aalto, 12 years after his death and after 30 years of planning history

1979 The Soviet Union invades Afghanistan

1939–1945 Second World War

1972 Beginning of construction of the
Centre Georges Pompidou in Paris

1993 The Maastricht Treaty takes effect,
formally establishing the European Union

1945 Atomic bombings of
Hiroshima and Nagasaki

1973 First oil crisis

1986 Chernobyl nuclear reactor disaster

2001 September 11 attacks

1910–1980 MODERNISM   POST-MODERNISM FROM 1980

1940   1945   1950   1955   1960   1965   1970   1975   1980   1985   1990   1995   2000   2005   2010   2015   2020   2025

ALVAR AALTO

Alvar Aalto wanted to be a painter. In the end he took up his career as an architect as a compromise with his parents. But his extraordinary creativity was not to be limited just to architecture, as can be seen in some 1,000 projects, including, along with many buildings, design icons such as the Aalto Vase.

For his first designs as an independent architect, Aalto fell back on the language of Neo-Classicism. But soon the young Finn, described as humorous and spontaneous, turned to new ideas. The buildings of Le Corbusier and the approaches of De Stijl and the Bauhaus left their traces in Finland too.

Teamwork

This stylistic transformation was not undertaken by the architect alone. For over 25 years Alvar Aalto worked together with his wife Aino, also an architect, who died in 1949. The tuberculosis sanatorium in Paimio, Finland, shows the Aaltos' altered approach around 1930: with their rows of windows, reinforced concrete and flat roofs the four different parts of the building are clearly derived from the rationalism of Le Corbusier, but they are organically joined together around the entrance area. Aalto also undertook the interior decoration of the sanatorium, and did so without exception: door handles and lamps, cupboards and chairs, are all based on his designs. Each detail was intended to contribute to the relaxation and convalescence of the patients.

Art and Technology

It was not so much his architectural designs as his furniture projects that cemented the Finn's reputation in Europe. His furniture was so successful that from 1935 the firm of Artek, specially founded for this purpose, undertook its production—which incidentally it does to this day. These successes were joined by further building projects: over the next decades Aalto designed a cellulose factory together with a residential estate, as well as private houses, churches and a university building, and the Finnish national pavilions at many international exhibitions. The Finnish architect's designs for these proved entirely individual: a curved wall, inclined forwards, adorned the Finnish exhibition pavilion at the New York World's Fair in 1939. The Technology University of Helsinki, begun by Aalto in 1949, is characterized on the outside by the use of red brick and granite. In the Main Hall, however, the impression is determined by concrete; moreover, the hall also fulfils its purpose when seen from the outside, as it forms the auditorium of an open-air theater. Aalto did not push himself forward as a theorist, yet his influence on later generations of architects and designers was immense. This was ensured by more than 300 assistants from all over the world who were employed by the Finn in the course of his long career.

1898 Born 3 February, in Kuortane, Finland
1916–21 Studies in Helsinki
1924 Marries the architect Aino Marsio
1928 Building for the newspaper *Turun Sanomat*, Turku, Finland
1929–32 Tuberculosis Sanatorium, Paimio, Finland
1933 Moves to Helsinki
1933–34 Exhibition of his furniture in London, Milan, Helsinki, and Zurich
1935 Foundation of the Artek company
1936–54 Cellulose factory and Sunila housing project in Kotka, Finland
1937 Finnish pavilion at the Paris World Exposition
1945–46 Teaches in the USA
1949 Death of his first wife. Work begins on building the Technology University of Helsinki
1952 Marries the architect Elissa Mäkiniemi
1976 Dies 11 May, in Helsinki, Finland

above
Today one of Helsinki's landmarks:
Aalto's Finlandia Hall

left
Slanting wall: the Finnish pavilion at
the New York World Exhibition of 1938

1881 * Pablo Picasso, Spanish artist, born

1886 Statue of Liberty,
New York

1872 Impression, Sunrise,
Claude Monet

1912 Wassily Kandinsky's *Concerning
the Spiritual In Art* is published

1914–1918 First World War

1901 * Alberto Giacometti, Swiss painter and sculptor, born

1840–1895 REVIVALISM   1895–1910 ART NOUVEAU   MODERNISM 1910–1980

1850 1855 1860 1865 1870 1875 1880 1885 1890 1895 1900 1905 1910 1915 1920 1925 1930 1935

The Bangladesh Parliament
building, Dhaka

WILLIAM VAN ALEN, AMERICAN ARCHITECT

FRANK LLOYD WRIGHT, AMERICAN ARCHITECT

1948 Assassination of
Mahatma Gandhi

1961 Berlin Wall erected   **1973** First oil crisis

1986 Chernobyl nuclear
reactor disaster

2001 September 11 attacks

1939–1945 Second World war

1963 John F. Kennedy assassination
in Dallas, Texas

1990 Final year of the Cold War era

1949 Birth of the People's
Republic of China

1910–1980 MODERNISM   POST-MODERNISM FROM 1980

1940   1945   1950   1955   1960   1965   1970   1975   1980   1985   1990   1995   2000   2005   2010   2015   2020   2025

LOUIS I. KAHN

Public housing, but also theaters and museums, churches, factories and office buildings—Louis Kahn was clearly capable of enthusiasm for all types of building projects. The American architect and teacher searched for a long time for his own style, but his search was to be rewarded.

The Russian-born Kahn, who at the age of five had already moved to Philadelphia with his family, studied architecture at the University of Pennsylvania. Armed with his diploma, he first worked in the office of the urban planner John Molitor in Philadelphia, to whose commission he built exhibition buildings in the Neo-Classical style. A journey to Europe followed in 1928–1929, during which Louis Kahn also revisited his birthplace. On his return to the East Coast of the United States, Kahn, newly married to Esther Israeli, was faced with the great Depression and worldwide economic crisis. Workless for many years, Kahn still pursued his ideas on architecture. The first opportunity to build finally presented itself in 1936. Kahn created an assembly building for the Ahavath Israel Congregation, whose unpretentiousness is impressive even from a distance: on the street side a massive block with brick cladding welcomes the visitor, with only three small windows in the stairwell breaking up the façade.

Clear Forms

The private houses executed by Kahn over the years that followed were presented with sharp edges and entirely without decoration. The choice of materials, however, was striking: the façades were given wooden cladding, the skirtings and walls are composed of ashlar. In 1951, on his 50th birthday, the architect received his first major commission, the extension to the Yale University art gallery. Kahn decided in favor of a clear contrast to the historic old building and built a block with quite different façades: a totally closed brick wall closes off the building on the street side, while the back is glazed and opens into a sculpture garden.

At Home and Abroad

Further large projects followed, as did honors and guest professorships. Kahn, however, often tried the patience of his clients, optimizing, altering, exploring new ideas (incidentally also in private, for he founded three families with three different women)—so that many of his designs never came into existence except on paper.

One that did, however, was the research building for medicine at Kahn's alma mater: the seven-story laboratory towers, three buildings on square ground plans, are grouped around a further square, which accommodates the central amenities. Kahn extended the ensemble to the west with two six-story laboratory towers for biological research, retaining the structure of the first building: the concrete load-bearing structure is recognizable in the brick façade, while all the edges of the towers terminate in glass. Kahn's laboratory building created a furor, and not only in the USA. In 1962 he gained two major commissions from Asia. In Ahmedabad in India he undertook the building of a commercial college. In Dhaka, he was given the responsibility for building the whole government district for the new capital. However, the first building for this project, the Parliament building, was not completed until nine years after Kahn's death.

1901 Born 20 February, in Saaremaa, Estonia (then Ösel, Russia)
1905 His family moves to Philadelphia
1920–24 Studies architecture at the University of Pennsylvania, Philadelphia
1930 Marries Esther Israeli
1951–53 Yale University Art Gallery
1955–57 Trenton Bathhouse, Trenton, New Jersey
1957 Becomes a professor at the University of Pennsylvania
1961–73 Fort Wayne Theater, Indiana
1962–75 Indian Institute of Management, Ahmedabad, India
1962–83 Bangladesh Parliament building, Dhaka
1966–72 Kimbell Art Museum, Fort Worth, Texas
1969–77 Yale Center for British Art, New Haven, Connecticut
1974 Dies 17 March, in New York

Louis I. Kahn's Salk Institute for Biological Research at La Jolla, California

WALTER GROPIUS, GERMAN ARCHITECT

LUDWIG MIES VAN DER ROHE, GERMAN ARCHITECT

MARCEL BREUER, AMERICAN ARCHITECT AND DESIGNER

1886 Statue of Liberty, New York

1883 First petrol-driven automobile,
Gottlieb Daimler and Carl Benz

1891 End of the Indian Wars in the USA

1912 * Jackson Pollock, American painter, born

1914–1918 First World war   **1928** * Andy Warhol,
American artist, b

1922 Howard Carter finds the entra
to King Tutankhamen's tomb
the Valley of the Kings

1840–1895 REVIVALISM   **1895–1910 ART NOUVEAU**   **MODERNISM 1910–1980**

| 1850 | 1855 | 1860 | 1865 | 1870 | 1875 | 1880 | 1885 | 1890 | 1895 | 1900 | 1905 | 1910 | 1915 | 1920 | 1925 | 1930 | 1935 |

1990 Final year of the Cold War era

1944 Allied troops land on the beaches
in Dallas, Texas
2001 September 11 attacks
of Normandy during D-Day

1963 John F. Kennedy assassination 1969 Neil Armstrong is the first person
to set foot on the Moon

1961 Berlin Wall erected   1973 First oil crisis   1986 Chernobyl nuclear reactor disaster

1939–1945 Second World War

1910–1980 MODERNISM   POST-MODERNISM FROM 1980

1940   1945   1950   1955   1960   1965   1970   1975   1980   1985   1990   1995   2000   2005   2010   2015   2020   2025

PHILIP JOHNSON

If there was a pop star of the architectural scene in the 20th century, it was Philip Johnson. His presence in the United States as critic, connoisseur, curator, but also architect, trendsetter and celebrity, has no equal.

Philip Johnson's name is linked above all with MoMA, the New York Museum of Modern Art. As first curator of architecture from 1930 to 1936 it was Johnson who introduced the Bauhaus architects such as Ludwig Mies van der Rohe, Marcel Breuer, and Walter Gropius to the American public and helped them to world celebrity. He himself achieved fame for the exhibition *The International Style* organized together with Henry-Russell Hitchcock, and also for his architecture from 1922 to 1936. His collaboration with Mies van der Rohe, to whom he devoted a whole exhibition at MoMA in 1947, and his close association with the museum, were both formed during those years.

Johnson studied philosophy and history, but during his first journeys through Europe he acquired a taste for architecture. This passion continued during his time as a critic and museum worker, and so at the age of 34 he began a study course in architecture in order to create buildings of his own. The first opportunity to do so was offered to him at MoMA in 1952, when he designed the Abby Aldrich Rockefeller sculpture garden in the inner courtyard. Some ten years later he again became actively involved with the extension of the museum and the sculpture garden.

Several of his buildings have enjoyed great fame, such as the Seagram Building with the Four Seasons Restaurant in New York, built together with Ludwig Mies van der Rohe, and his own residence: the Glass House (1949) in New Canaan is a fascinating low-level building based on projects by Mies van der Rohe. It is essentially a glass box on a brick base: a steel construction with a flat roof, glass walls and a brick cylinder in the interior, which accommodates the bathroom and fireplace. This building, which lies in the middle of a park with further, very varied works by Johnson, places the living space in the heart of nature. Today it is a protected building. The headquarters of AT&T (now the Sony Plaza high-rise) was also to be an emblematic building.

This is a stone structure in a rose-gray color unusual for the 1980s, with a curved pediment whose form is historically inspired. It soon acquired the nickname of the Chippendale Building.

In addition to his own building activity, Johnson never lost sight of the architecture of others, and so, at the age of 80, he helped present contemporary avant-garde styles to the public in the exhibition *Deconstructivist Architecture*. Under this label, which is still used today, were featured the offices of Coop Himmelb(l)au, Peter Eisenman, Frank Gehry, Rem Koolhaas, Daniel Libeskind, Bernard Tschumi, and Zaha Hadid.

Rarely has an architect made use of such a wide variety of forms, something that has often been criticized in Johnson. He rose above such objections with irony and ready wit; for him, it was only a good dose of provocation that gave flavor to a debate. His burning interest in architecture and his eclectic inspiration, coupled with his social presence, made him one of the most colorful personalities in 20th-century New York.

1906 Born 8 July, in Cleveland, Ohio
1930–36 Becomes the founder and director of the Department of Architecture at the Museum of Modern Art in New York
1932 Curates the exhibition *The International Style: Architecture Since 1922*
1940 Begins a course of study at Harvard under Walter Gropius and Marcel Breuer
1946–54 Again director of the Department of Architecture at MoMA
1947 Crates the exhibition *Mies van der Rohe*
1949 Glass House, his own residence, New Canaan, Connecticut
1952 Extension and sculpture garden, MoMA
1954–58 Seagram Building, with Ludwig Mies van der Rohe
1967–87 Opens office with John Burgee
1976 Pennzoil Plaza, Houston, Texas
1978–84 AT&T high-rise (now Sony Plaza), New York
1979 Awarded the Pritzker Prize
1988 Curates the exhibition *Deconstructivist Architecture*
1990 Crystal Cathedral, Garden Grove, California
2005 Dies 25 January, in New Canaan

The Glass House – a building bounded by nature

LE CORBUSIER, SWISS ARCHITECT

LÚCIO COSTA, BRASILIAN ARCHITECT

FRANK O. GEHRY, CANADIAN-AMERICAN ARCHITECT

1886 Statue of Liberty, New York

1883 First petrol-driven automobile,
Gottlieb Daimler and Carl Benz

1891 End of the Indian Wars in the USA

1914–1918 First World war

1912 * Jackson Pollock,
American painter,
born

1924 Summer Olympics openi
ceremonies held in Paris

1840–1895 REVIVALISM   **1895–1910 ART NOUVEAU**   **MODERNISM 1910–1980**

| 1850 | 1855 | 1860 | 1865 | 1870 | 1875 | 1880 | 1885 | 1890 | 1895 | 1900 | 1905 | 1910 | 1915 | 1920 | 1925 | 1930 | 1935 |

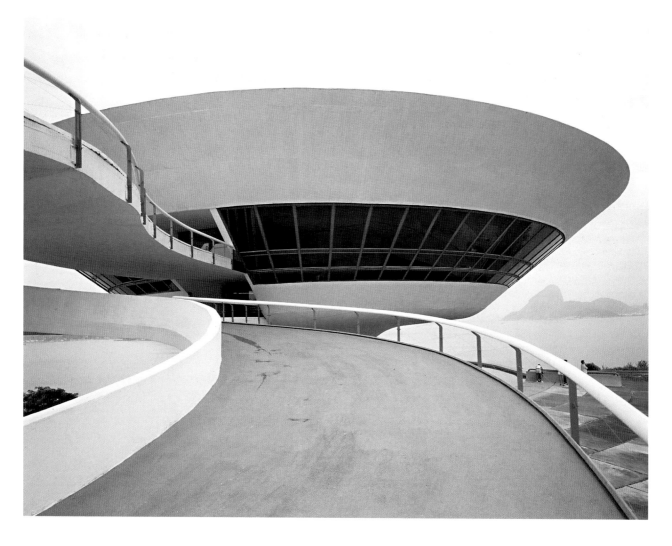

Museum for Contemporary Art
(Museu de Arte Contemporânea)
in Niterói near Rio de Janeiro

World Fair in Paris
1939–1945 Second World War

1961 Berlin Wall erected
1964 21 years of dictatorship in Brazil begin

1969 Neil Armstrong is the first person to set foot on the Moon
1973 First oil crisis

1986 Chernobyl nuclear reactor disaster
1990 Final year of the Cold War era
2001 September 11 attacks

1910–1980 MODERNISM   POST-MODERNISM   FROM 1980

1940   1945   1950   1955   1960   1965   1970   1975   1980   1985   1990   1995   2000   2005   2010   2015   2020   2025

OSCAR NIEMEYER

A better backdrop for science fiction films could hardly be imagined. Around a circular building, an elegant, weightless arc rises through the air against a blue sky; on the beach a UFO seems to have landed; and a white sphere comes to earth in the middle of Paris.

These serpentine, futuristic buildings all bear the same, unmistakable hallmarks of a living myth: Oscar Niemeyer, born a hundred years ago.

Since his childhood he has been drawing, at that time with his finger held up to the sky, today at his drawing board in his office near the Copacabana in Rio de Janeiro.

World-famous as architect of the city of Brasilia, he has remained a supporter of revolutionary ideals—the revolution of the curve against the right angle, and the Marxist revolution for a better world. Social justice, independence of capitalism, these are the great aims to whose pursuit Niemeyer allows greater importance than to architecture: "The most important thing is life. Sometimes I think that a young man demonstrating on the street is doing more important work than I am."

When Niemeyer completed his education in the mid-1930s, he had the good luck to be able to take part straight away in an important project, working closely with Le Corbusier and learnt from him. The latter came to Brazil for three months, and between 1936 and 1943 the Health and Education Ministry came into being in Rio de Janeiro. Niemeyer's collaboration with this distinguished colleague was repeated some years later with the headquarters of the United Nations in New York.

In Brazil Niemeyer was soon offered important public commissions: after the mayor of the city, and future president of the country, Juscelino Kubitschek, had entrusted to him the design of the Pampulha district in Belo Horizonte, there followed the legendary project—the creation of a new city. Together with Lucio Costa, Niemeyer was commissioned to create out of nothing a new capital city for Brazil, Brasilia. The urban planner Costa placed on the drawing board the plan, divided by function, in which later the breathtaking concrete buildings found their places, like sculptures in an exhibition. The Catedral Metropolitana, the Congress Building with Senate and House of Representatives, and the Supreme Court in Brasilia are icons of modern building. The living accommodation in this futuristic city is controversial. Since 1987 it has been under the protection of UNESCO as a World Cultural Heritage site. Niemeyer himself believes that a visit to Brasilia could arouse different reactions, but no one could be indifferent to it. For him, this is exactly what architecture was about.

At the beginning of the new millennium he enhanced Brasilia with the National Museum, a characteristic white concrete dome with a free-floating ramp—it looks for all the world like a B-movie space ship.

In Niterói, on the side of the bay facing Rio de Janeiro, lies a whole Niemeyer promenade, or Caminho Niemeyer: a complex with a theater and a museum for contemporary art. Altogether it is to comprise 12 buildings, the greatest assembly of Niemeyer's architecture outside Brasilia.

In the course of his long career, Oscar Niemeyer has worked on more than 500 projects. His creed is beauty and surprise through free and sensual form for the enrichment of life. He has never subjected himself to the dictatorship of the right angle, but invokes the inspiring forms of nature, such as mountains and waves.

When 100 years old, Niemeyer remarried, and today, smoking a cigar, he enters his office daily, where his grandchildren and great-grandchildren support him in the translation of his design sketches into actual buildings.

1907 Born 15 December, in Rio de Janeiro, Brazil

1934 Receives his diploma from the Escola Nacional de Belas Artes in Rio

1936–45 Takes part in designing the Health and Education Ministry, symbol of Brazilian Modernism

1940–43 Church of San Francisco, Pampulha/Belo Horizonte

1945 Joins the Brazilian Communist Party

1947 With Le Corbusier, designs the headquarters of the United Nations in New York

1955–70 Design the building of the new capital Brasilia, with Lucio Costa

(1964–85 Military dictatorship in Brazil)

1965 Exiled in France, he meets André Malraux and Jean-Paul Sartre and builds the headquarters of the Communist Party of France

1968 Mondadori Publishers building, Milan

1988 Pritzker Prize

1991 Museum of Contemporary Art (Museu de Arte Contemporânea), the "Flying Saucer," in Niterói, Brazil

2002 Oscar Niemeyer Museum (Museu Oscar Niemeyer), in Curitiba, Brazil

2003 Summer pavilion of the Serpentine Gallery, London

Views of the Congress Building and
the towers of the Supreme Federal
Court in Brasília

ALVAR AALTO, FINISH ARCHITECT AND DESIGNER

CHARLES EAMES, AMERICAN DESIGNER

1886 Statue of Liberty, New York

1891 End of the Indian Wars in the USA

1914–1918 First World war

1883 First petrol-driven automobile,
Gottlieb Daimler and Carl Benz

1928 * Andy Warhol,
American artist
born

1929 Start of the
Great
Depression

1840–1895 REVIVALISM   1895–1910 ART NOUVEAU   MODERNISM 1910–1980

| 1850 | 1855 | 1860 | 1865 | 1870 | 1875 | 1880 | 1885 | 1890 | 1895 | 1900 | 1905 | 1910 | 1915 | 1920 | 1925 | 1930 | 1935 |

left
Commissioned for large-scale industry:
the General Motors Technical Center

below
The "spirit of flying" is manifested in
Saarinen's TWA Terminal at John F.
Kennedy International Airport

STEVEN HOLL, AMERICAN ARCHITECT

1939–1945 Second World War   **1950** India becomes a republic   **1969** Neil Armstrong is the first person to set foot on the Moon   **2001** September 11 attacks

1942 Beginning of construction of   **1960** John F. Kennedy becomes US president
Idlewild Airport, later renamed   **1961** Berlin Wall erected   **1973** First oil crisis   **1990** Final year of the Cold War era
John F. Kennedy International
Airport, New York   **1910–1980 MODERNISM   POST-MODERNISM FROM 1980**

1940   1945   1950   1955   1960   1965   1970   1975   1980   1985   1990   1995   2000   2005   2010   2015   2020   2025

EERO SAARINEN

Eero Saarinen said of himself that he had "grown up under the drawing board." With an architect father, he had the best possible chance of learning the trade in his early years, becoming one of America's most original designers.

Eero Saarinen's career is closely linked to that of his father, the architect Eliel Saarinen. In 1923 the family emigrated from Finland to the United States, and it was there that Eero Saarinen created some of the iconic images of 20th century architecture.

After completing his education, which included studying sculpture in Paris, Eero Saarinen joined his father's firm. After the latter's death in 1950 he continued to run it on his own. Eero Saarinen spent an important part of his early working years at the artists' colony Cranbrook, a park campus in Michigan dedicated to the arts. The commission to build this complex, including an academy, artists' workshops, a museum and library, had gone to his father in 1925. For several years the whole family was involved with this project. Eero concluded his study of architecture at Yale in 1934, and then traveled for two years through Europe and the Middle East. On his return, father and son founded Saarinen & Saarinen, and worked from Cranbrook until 1942.

In 1940, a team of artists working at Cranbrook with Eero Saarinen and the designer Charles Eames, won two first prizes in a competition on *Organic Design for Domestic Furniture* sponsored by the New York Museum of Modern Art. Over the years that followed, Eero Saarinen designed and produced furniture strongly influenced by these projects. In doing so, he also experimented with materials that contrasted strongly with the natural materials of the Arts and Crafts Movement, which had greatly influenced his youth: he now turned to fiberglass, plastic, aluminum, chrome, steel, and leather. Together with Eames, in 1945 Saarinen designed two model houses that also used new, light and industrial building materials and combinable, flexible modules.

One of Saarinen's most important projects, and at the same time one of the largest postwar commissions, was the building of the General Motors Technical Center: when it was completed after eight years, the architectural firm had quintupled in size.

The complex is designed around a square artificial lake, with buildings distributed around it of various sizes in the form of boxes, with glass or porcelain façades suspended in front of them.

"General Motors is a metal-working industry; a precision industry; a mass production industry. Thus, the design is based on steel, the metal of the automobile, like the automobile itself, the buildings are essentially put together as on an assembly line, out of mass-produced units. And, down to the smallest detail, we tried to give the architecture the precise, well made look which is a proud characteristic of industrial America."

The complex was a stunning success, and resulted in many further commissions for Saarinen, including the premises of IBM in Rochester (1956–1958), and the technologically and formally innovative headquarters of Deere & Company in Moline, Illinois (1956–1964), with an elegant façade of pre-rusted steel and glass.

In addition to these industrial buildings with their practical, clearly geometric forms, Saarinen created two structures based on circular forms on the campus of the Massachusetts Institute of Technology in Cambridge, Massachusetts: the chapel is a windowless brick cylinder, the auditorium a spherical concrete shell, more precisely a triangular section of an eighth of a sphere. The form stands on the ground at three points, with glass façades inserted between roof and floor.

Probably Saarinen's best-known building is the TransWorld Airlines (TWA) Terminal at John F. Kennedy Airport in New York. Between 1956 and 1962 a dynamic structure was created here from curved concrete shells, offering passengers beneath its sweeping roof effective routes, generously proportioned lounges and—through glass façades—a broad view of the runways. In common with Dulles International Airport in Washington, to which it is also related in other ways, it has a dynamic wave form, conveying the idea of flying.

1910 Born 20 August, in Kirkkonummi, Finland
1923 His family moves to Detroit
1929–30 Studies sculpture in Paris
1934 Receives his diploma in architecture from Yale
1934–36 Travels through Europe
1937–50 Works with his father, Eliel Saarinen
1940 Becomes an American citizen
1948 Designs the Jefferson National Expansion Memorial, St. Louis, realized in 1963 as Gateway Arch
1948–56 Builds General Motors Technical Center in Warren, Michigan
1950–61 Continues to run his office, in addition to furniture design
1954–55 Chapel and Kresge Auditorium of MIT (Massachusetts Institute of Technology)
1956–63 TransWorld Airlines Terminal, John F. Kennedy International Airport, New York
1958–62 Dulles International Airport (for Washington)
1961 Dies 1 September, in Ann Arbor, Michigan

1883 First petrol-driven automobile,
Gottlieb Daimler and Carl Benz

1868 Shogun Tokugawa
Yoshinobu surrenders

1886 Statue of Liberty, New York

1914-1918 First World war

1929 Start of the G
Depression
1931 Wakatsu
jiro resig
Prime M
of Japan

1840–1895 REVIVALISM   1895–1910 ART NOUVEAU   MODERNISM 1910–1980

1850 1855 1860 1865 1870 1875 1880 1885 1890 1895 1900 1905 1910 1915 1920 1925 1930 1935

7 *Guernica*, Pablo Picasso   **1948** Assassination of Mahatma Gandhi

1941 Japanese attack on Pearl Harbor   **1961** Berlin Wall erected   **1973** First oil crisis   **1990** German reunification

1945 Atomic bombings of   **1949** Birth of the People's Republic of China

Hiroshima and Nagasaki   **1965** Nobel Prize (Peace) for United Nation's Children's Fund (UNICEF)   **2001** September 11 attacks

1939–1945 Second World War

1910–1980 MODERNISM   POST-MODERNISM FROM 1980

1940   1945   1950   1955   1960   1965   1970   1975   1980   1985   1990   1995   2000   2005   2010   2015   2020   2025

KENZO TANGE

The name Kenzo Tange is emblematic of Japan's new beginning after the Second World War. In Hiroshima, the place of the greatest catastrophe, at 36 years old and at the beginning of his career, he built the peace memorial, an important symbol for Japan and the world. History and architecture, tradition and the future were linked in his work from this moment on.

The Hiroshima Peace Memorial Park marks the spot where the atom bomb fell. On the site of the destruction, the present-day park with its space for great numbers of visitors, stands the concrete memorial designed by Kenzo Tange, whose high arched form is related both to that of the bomb and of a traditional Japanese house. The nearby Peace Center is a long linear building in concrete on columns. This sober form takes account of its purpose; at the same time it allows us to recognize the influence of an important source of inspiration for the architect, namely that of Le Corbusier.

Apart from the work of Le Corbusier, Kenzo Tange had devoted himself intensively to questions of urban planning. The meaning of people's daily journeys to work and back, the transport routes within a city, fascinated him in particular. In 1960 he proposed a plan for the development and structuring of Tokyo, which provided for the extension across the harbor, by means of bridges and artificial islands, of this city by the sea. The solutions he sketched out for the future of the overfilled and rapidly expanding city are still being discussed today.

Although his plans for urban extension into the harbor have remained unexecuted, the cityscape of Tokyo bears Tange's unmistakable stamp. Among his most famous buildings are the two sport halls for the 1964 Olympics. Their semicircular, curved roofs with their elegant and memorable forms are suspended on steel cables, and looking at them one is easily reminded of a ship's hulk or a temple building, the shape of a comma or of a leaf. A further landmark is Tokyo's city hall. In 1991 the prefecture government moved into this building, whose two high-rise towers are centrally linked by a lower-level building. This building is a symbol of the important government tasks of the vast, present-day city, and at the same time recalls the contours of a cathedral.

Another of Tokyo's sights is the headquarters of the Fuji Company, whose almost airy structure consists of bridges and struts between two huge towers. Its distinguishing mark is the sphere that sits at the highest level, which gives the building, almost entirely clad with aluminum, a playfully futuristic touch.

The destruction wrought by the Second World War brought the opportunity for young architects to replace the lost buildings with new forms. Kenzo Tange seized this chance eagerly, thus significantly contributing to the architectural image of today's Japan. While he himself emphasized the importance of Le Corbusier for his work, he combined this influence with that of Japanese architectural tradition, using his forms and materials—above all concrete—with the greatest of skill. Japan's tradition-conscious view of the future is reflected in his work.

As a teacher, Kenzo Tange was active not only in Japan, but also as a guest professor in the United States. Among his best-known students are the noted architects Fumihiko Maki, Kisho Kurokawa, and Arato Isozaki.

1913 Born 4 September, in Imabari, Shikoku Island, Japan
1938 Receives his diploma from the University of Tokyo
1942–45 Further studies
FROM 1946 Teaches
1946 A member of a committee for the reconstruction of Japan, he develops plan for a new Hiroshima, and builds the Peace Memorial
1960 Plan for Tokyo
1964 Sports halls for Tokyo Olympics
1965 Awarded the RIBA (Royal Institute of British Architects) Gold Medal
1965 St Mary's Cathedral, Tokyo
1987 Awarded Pritzker Prize
1991 Tokyo City Hall
1996 Fuji TV Building, Tokyo
2005 Dies 22 March, in Tokyo

Austere simplicity: Tange's administrative building for the Kagawa prefecture in Takamatsu

above
Tange's memorial for the victims of the
atom bomb attack on Hiroshima

right
St Mary's Cathedral is the seat of the
archdiocese of Tokyo

LUDWIG MIES VAN DER ROHE, GERMAN ARCHITECT

KENZO TANGE, JAPANESE ARCHITECT

ARATA ISOZAKI, JAPANESE ARCHITECT

1900 Boxer Rebellion in China

1856–1860 The Second Opium War
between several western powers
and China begins

1893 * Mao Zedong, Chinese military
and political leader, born

1914–1918 First World war

1929 Start of the
Great Depressi

1931 Wakatsuk
jiro resign
Prime Min
of Japan

1840–1895 REVIVALISM   **1895–1910 ART NOUVEAU**   **MODERNISM 1910–1980**

| 1850 | 1855 | 1860 | 1865 | 1870 | 1875 | 1880 | 1885 | 1890 | 1895 | 1900 | 1905 | 1910 | 1915 | 1920 | 1925 | 1930 | 1935 |

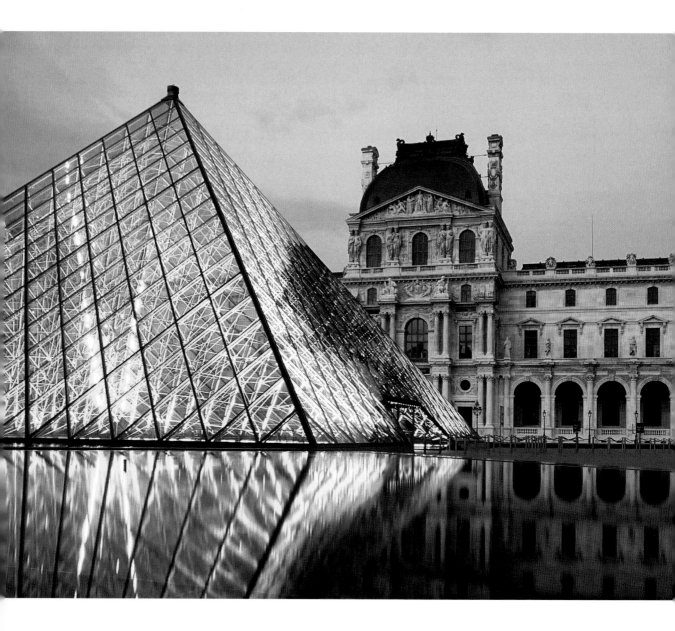

1939–1945 Second World War 1949 Birth of the People's Republic of China 1989 Tiananmen Square massacre, Beijing 2008 Summer Olympics take place in Beijing

1948 The World Health Organization is established by the United Nations

1948 United Nations General Assembly adopts Universal Declaration of Human Rights

1965 Nobel Prize (Peace) for United Nation's Children's Fund (UNICEF)

1959 Frank Lloyd Wright's Guggenheim Museum is completed

1994 South Africa holds its first fully multiracial elections

2001 September 11 attacks

1910–1980 MODERNISM   POST-MODERNISM FROM 1980

1940 1945 1950 1955 1960 1965 1970 1975 1980 1985 1990 1995 2000 2005 2010 2015 2020 2025

IEOH MING PEI

Who can think of the Louvre today and not see the glass pyramids by the Chinese-born American architect I.M. Pei that stand in its inner courtyards? While the architectural ensemble can no longer be imagined without them, their creation was for a long time marked by polemics about the extension of the Louvre. As one of President François Mitterrand's prestige projects, it was realized by means of efficient diplomacy in the face of great public resistance.

In the former royal palace, and today museum, of the Louvre, a large glass pyramid was built in the Cour Napoléon, through which the museum is entered. From here there is access to the gallery spaces, as well as the underground passages with cloakroom, cash desk, shops, and cafés. It is to the rebuilding by I.M. Pei, in particular the roofing over of interior courtyards, that the museum owes a significantly greater surface area. Smaller pyramids and an inverted pyramid over the atrium of the underground shopping arcade attached to the museum complete the work. The complex of the Grand Louvre, with its pool by day and effective lighting by night, remains a popular venue.

Before this, his masterwork, Pei had already completed another important museum extension. The east wing of the National Gallery of Art in Washington was opened in 1978 after ten years' work on the project. Here an H-shaped, solid structure lies opposite the older museum. The interior rooms are on different levels and are linked by stairs and a central, triangular atrium. The museum is lit through skylights, and the atrium lies under a glass roof composed of pyramids.

The triangle and pyramid are characteristic elements in Pei's buildings. In the Bank of China in Hong Kong, completed by Pei in 1990, they are linked in a particular way. The bank headquarters are accommodated in a high-rise building of mirror glass whose whole structure is based on the triangle. Four tower units are arranged in staggered formation with pyramidal sloping roofs, creating one of the most widely visible buildings of Hong Kong. The symbolic ambition of this skyscraper was no less than to announce the economic liberalization of China.

In Germany, I.M. Pei was again commissioned to build an extension to an important museum: the German History Museum in Berlin has been considerably enlarged by the new exhibition galleries, again in a triangular building. From the old building, whose inner courtyard Pei had roofed over with steel and glass, one reaches the new museum spaces by means of an underground passage. The glass stairwell in the form of a spindle is the essential feature of the new structure, which is in direct proximity to works by an architect of the past admired by Pei, Karl Friedrich Schinkel (see page 39).

Pei had come to the United States from China as a young man. He began his career as architect after the Second World War, opening his own office in New York at the age of 38. Since then, with a number of cultural institutions, but also with high-rise buildings, he has attained his declared target: "I carry in me the great wish to leave something behind. This has nothing to do with ego. I believe one owes it to one's own existence to leave something behind that will last."

1917 Born Ieoh Ming Pei, 26 April, in Canton, China
1935 Arrives in the USA
1940 Graduates from Massachusetts Institute of Technology
1942 Studies with Gropius at Harvard
1946 Receives his diploma in architecture from Harvard
1946–55 Works with William Zeckendorf
1954 Becomes an American citizen
1955–66 I.M. Pei & Associates formed
1964–79 John F. Kennedy Library, Boston
1966–89 I. M. Pei & Partners
1968–78 Extension to the National Gallery of Art, Washington
1982–90 Bank of China, Hong Kong
1983 Awarded the Pritzker Prize
1989–1990 Pei Cobb Freed & Partners formed
1988–93 Rebuilding and pyramids at Louvre
1997–2003 Extension to German History Museum, Berlin

It gave a new face to the Louvre: Pei's glass pyramid, forming the entrance to the museum

above
The east wing of the National Gallery
of Art in Washington

right
High-rise in mirror glass: the Bank
of China in Hong Kong

1872 *Impression, Sunrise,* Claude Monet   **1914–1918** First World war   **1929** Start of the Great Depression

1866 * Wassily Kandinsky, Russian artist, born   **1881** * Pablo Picasso, Spanish artist, born

1840–1895 REVIVALISM   1895–1910 ART NOUVEAU   MODERNISM 1910–1980

| 1850 | 1855 | 1860 | 1865 | 1870 | 1875 | 1880 | 1885 | 1890 | 1895 | 1900 | 1905 | 1910 | 1915 | 1920 | 1925 | 1930 | 1935 |

The roof landscape of the Olympic stadium recalls the shoreline of the Olympic Lake

| 1939–1945 Second World War | 1961 Berlin Wall erected | 1972 Summer Olympics take place in Munich |

1944 Allied troops land on the beaches of Normandy during D-Day
1963 John F. Kennedy assassination in Dallas, Texas
2001 September 11 attacks

1946 First meeting of the United Nations
1990 German reunification

1969 Neil Armstrong is the first person to set foot on the Moon

1949 Democratic Republic of Germany DDR established officially

1910–1980 MODERNISM   POST-MODERNISM FROM 1980

1940   1945   1950   1955   1960   1965   1970   1975   1980   1985   1990   1995   2000   2005   2010   2015   2020   2025

GÜNTER BEHNISCH

Two impressions have remained in the public memory of the Munich Olympics of 1972: the terrorist attack on the one hand, the optimistically swinging "tent roof" over the Olympiapark on the other. This was designed by Günther Behnisch, and is to this day inseparable from the image of Munich, an image of the triumph of the human spirit over tragedy.

In 1972, when Germany invited sports people from all over the world to the Summer Olympics, the intention was to make a new German identity tangible internationally. This was also expressed by the light, open tent structure of the roofing, which Behnisch had designed and executed. In terms of engineering technology, the construction of a tent roof that was to stretch over the stadium, the sports hall and the swimming pool was a huge challenge. That this approach was successful is shown by the unbroken popularity of the Olympiapark to this day. In 1990 Behnisch's Museum for Communication was opened in Frankfurt. The building is dominated by a glass semi-cone, by which the interior is generously supplied with daylight. Steel, glass, and wood give lightness to the museum, and the open spaces and large window areas convey the concept of "open communication." Since 2007, the museum can also be seen via the virtual world Second Life.

The Plenary Hall built in Bonn in 1992, before the move of the Bundestag to Berlin, is also intended to demonstrate openness, and to dispel distancing aura of political authority: Behnisch saw the hall as a workspace rather than a building designed to impress the public, and so it is both technologically advanced and devoid of pretentiousness of any kind. Observable from outside, it symbolizes the principle of democratic surveillance of the government's work, and the closeness of the government to the electorate. Today, after the change in capital, the hall is the centerpiece of the new World Conference Center in Bonn.

Openness is also the watchword of Behnisch's most recent Berlin building, the Academy of Arts on Pariser Platz close to the Brandenburg Gate. This was completed in 2005 after eleven years' work by Behnisch & Partner with Werner Durth. In the interior of the glass façade of the building, the remnants of the old Academy building, in particular the historic skylit halls of the Palais Arnim-Boitzenburg, are preserved. Staircases, ramps and bridges of steel and glass dominate the interior of the new structure. Here, as he does in general, Behnisch turns away from the monumental stone architecture that he firmly rejects, particularly for ideological reasons.

With his urban structures, schools, and other public buildings, Günther Behnisch has made his mark on postwar architecture in the Federal Republic of Germany, and thus taken up a position in favor of an open and unpretentious manner of building and mentality. The library of the University of Eichstätt is among his most important works in this area. The architect has clearly distanced himself from the heavy, rigid forms that belong to the political past. This is reflected in his attitude to planning: "I feel one cannot and should not regulate everything. Otherwise what you get in the end is a sort of prescriptive architecture, which tries to control everything. No, in my houses there can be contradictions, they do not necessarily have to be right. They are open to many things, including alterations to themselves."

1922 Born 12 June, in Dresden, Germany
1947–51 Studies architecture at the Technische Hochschule, Stuttgart
1951–52 Works with Rolf Gutbrod
1952 Founds his own office
1967 Teaches at the Technische Hochschule, Darmstadt
1968 Teaches at the Technische Hochschule, Stuttgart
1968–72 Olympiapark, Munich
1980–87 Central Library of the Catholic University, Eichstätt
1990 Museum for Communication, Frankfurt
1992 Plenary Hall of the German Bundestag, Bonn
2005 Academy of Arts, Berlin

The Museum of Fantasy of the collector Lothar-Günther Buchheim in Bernried near Munich

OSCAR NIEMEYER, BRASILIAN ARCHITECT

RAFFAEL MONEO, SPANISH ARCHITECT

EERO SAARINEN, FINISH ARCHITECT

1886 Statue of Liberty, New York

1907 *Les Demoiselles d'Avignon,*
Pablo Picasso

1928 * Andy Warhol,
American artist, born

1883 First petrol-driven automobile,
Gottlieb Daimler and Carl Benz

1914–1918 First
World war

1929 Start of the Great Depr

1931 Empire State Buildi
the highest buildin
the world

1840–1895 REVIVALISM   **1895–1910 ART NOUVEAU**   **MODERNISM 1910–1980**

1850   1855   1860   1865   1870   1875   1880   1885   1890   1895   1900   1905   1910   1915   1920   1925   1930   1935

The Petronas Towers in Kuala Lumpur
were long considered the tallest
building in the world

1939–1945 Second World War

1948 United Nations General Assembly adopts Universal Declaration of Human Rights

1950 India forms a republic

1963 John F. Kennedy assassination in Dallas, Texas

1967 Six-Day war in the Middle East

1969 Neil Armstrong is the first person to set foot on the Moon

1974 Juan Perón, Argentine President, dies

1986 Chernobyl nuclear reactor disaster

1990 German reunification

1997 Frank O. Gehry's Guggenheim Museum Bilbao is completed

2001 September 11 attacks

2003 Third Gulf War (US invasion of Iraq)

1910–1980 MODERNISM   POST-MODERNISM FROM 1980

1940 1945 1950 1955 1960 1965 1970 1975 1980 1985 1990 1995 2000 2005 2010 2015 2020 2025

CESAR PELLI

The building of towers—not in Babel, but worldwide—is one of the main tasks of the firm of Pelli Clarke Pelli, founded by Cesar Pelli when he was 41 years old. Today his towers stand in Europe, North America, Asia, and South America.

"Why do we build tall buildings? Very tall constructions have been built with great effort in almost all cultures all over the world. The urge to build as high as possible seems to be a basic characteristic of human culture." Of course Cesar Pelli is familiar with the Tower of Babel: "What interests me most in the Bible story is that the human desire to build as high as possible into the sky seemed to its authors to be universal." Nothing has changed to this day. Cesar Pelli has become famous, among other things, for the most recent high-rise record before the new millennium: his twin towers in Kuala Lumpur were, at 452 meters, the tallest building in the world. Built up into the sky in forms inspired by Islam, the two skyscrapers, which are linked about halfway up by a skywalk, form a gate. Their steel and glass façades are colored gold by the sunlight. There was a thoroughly symbolic significance in the fact that these two towers brought Kuala Lumpur and Malaysia into the 21st century.

A not uncontroversial tower was created in the center of New York when, in the late 1970s, Cesar Pelli received the commission to add an extension to the famous Museum of Modern Art, MoMA. Since the opening of the museum in 1939 it had been rebuilt in several stages. Pelli enlarged the west wing and gave it a graduated glass façade. In addition, he added a tower to the museum, of which only the lower ten floors were used directly by MoMA. The exhibition areas were doubled, but the museum's strategy in improving its finances by means of the new apartments and offices was criticized, and Cesar Pelli with it.

Of course, the architect has not built only towers. His first post already brought interesting tasks along with it, for at barely 30 years of age Cesar Pelli was working with Eero Saarinen on projects such as the TWA airport terminal in New York, and the Dulles International Airport in Washington. Both buildings are icons of the American architecture of their time. Also in Washington, Pelli's extension of Ronald Reagan Airport was opened in 1997: a longitudinal building, highly rhythmic as a result of the rounded arches of the roof, in whose interior great value is placed on the orientation and well-being of the passengers. Large window fronts offer a view of the nearby river, and light-flooded halls are adorned by artworks integrated by Pelli in the overall design.

In 2004, the National Museum of Art was opened in Osaka, a building that is the opposite of tall: here, under an eccentric sculptural formation, the exhibition galleries lie three floors below ground. This has given the museum the nickname of "the submarine." The projecting steel formation above ground accommodates the entrance area of the museum in a glass structure. This striking construction has become an important component of the cityscape of Osaka and its art quarter.

A specialist in tall buildings with offbeat surfaces, Pelli also demonstrates the profundity of his thought with lower-lying projects.

1926 Born 12 October, in Tucuman, Argentina

1949 Receives his diploma in architecture from the University of Tucuman, followed by further study in Illinois

1954–64 Works with Eero Saarinen

1964–68 Works with Daniel, Mann, Johnson and Mendenhall

1968–74 Works with Gruen Associates

1974–76 City Hall, San Bernardino

1976 Pacific Design Center, Los Angeles

1977 Founds his own firm, Pelli Clarke Pelli Architects

1977–84 Serves as dean of Yale University School of Architecture

1977–84 Museum of Modern Art, extension and renovation, New York

1990–97 Washington National Airport, new terminal

1993–98 Petronas Towers, Kuala Lumpur, Malaysia

2004 National Museum of Art, Osaka

CHARLES EAMES, AMERICAN DESIGNER

1883 First petrol-driven automobile,
Gottlieb Daimler and Carl Benz

1914–1918 First World war

1928 * Andy Warhol,
American artist
born

1886 Statue of Liberty, New York

1891 End of the Indian Wars in the USA

1929 Great
Depression

1840–1895 REVIVALISM   **1895–1910 ART NOUVEAU   MODERNISM 1910–1980**

1850   1855   1860   1865   1870   1875   1880   1885   1890   1895   1900   1905   1910   1915   1920   1925   1930   1935

7 *Guernica,*
Pablo Picasso

1939–1945 Second
World War

1948 The World Health Organization is established by the
United Nations

1948 United Nations General
Assembly adopts Universal
Declaration of Human Rights

1959 Frank Lloyd Wright's Guggenheim Museum is completed

1961 Berlin Wall erected

1965 Nobel Prize (Peace) for United Nation's Children's Fund (UNICEF)

1986 Chernobyl nuclear reactor disaster

1990 German reunification

1993 The Maastricht Treaty takes effect, formally
establishing the European Union

2001 September 11 attacks

1910–1980 MODERNISM   POST-MODERNISM FROM 1980

1940   1945   1950   1955   1960   1965   1970   1975   1980   1985   1990   1995   2000   2005   2010   2015   2020   2025

FRANK O. GEHRY

What architect, what client or mayor does not dream of achieving a "Bilbao effect" with his building? Since 1997, when the Guggenheim Museum lifted the Spanish harbor city out of its industrial misery and insignificance and transformed it into a tourist attraction, attempts have been made worldwide to copy the concept of the "specific upgrading of places through spectacular buildings by star architects" (Wikipedia).

Many, for the sake of simplicity, have gone straight to the Bilbao architect himself—Frank Gehry. Gehry was by no means unknown when he was commissioned to design the museum. As early as 1989 he had been awarded the Pritzker Prize, the "Nobel Prize for Architecture." But he was an awkward customer. If you wanted conventional building forms, you would not turn to him. For Gehry, architecture is art combined with a desire to push materials and techniques to new limits.

Architecture As Art

Frank Owen Gehry was born on in Toronto, Canada, in 1929. In 1947 he moved to California, took the most varied jobs and studied architecture at the University of Southern California until 1954, and later urban development at the Harvard Graduate School of Design. It was not until 1962 that he founded his first office in Los Angeles, today called Gehry Partners LLP, with more than 175 staff. The master, however, continues to make his designs himself: models in cardboard and metalized paper, folded, crumpled, tried out and abandoned again until the shape is right and promises enough tension and effectiveness. That these little paper sculptures can be turned into buildings, into museums or concert halls, whose gravity seems to have become suspended, is thanks to a sophisticated 3-D computer program that was originally developed for the aircraft industry. With this program it is possible to calculate not only the statics of the buildings but also the material costs and production processes, and to optimize the client's specifications. Though Gehry can be a controversial architect, his buildings are kept within the agreed time frame and budget.

Deconstructivism

Gehry's style of building has continued to develop from the early 1970s to today with an unbroken record of openness to new ideas. By using unusual, supposedly "poor" materials such as plywood and corrugated iron—today they are concrete and titanium—and breaking through traditional vocabularies of form, with the introduction of a fragmented geometry of oblique and split levels, canted spaces, slits, folds and distortions, Gehry comes across as the representative par excellence of Deconstructivism. And in fact he is one of the seven architects brought together by Philip Johnson in 1988 for the *Deconstructivist Architecture* exhibition at the New York Museum of Modern Art, who for the first time applied this philosophical concept to architecture. Gehry himself rejects all categorization, but with or without a label he will go down in architectural history.

1929 Born on 28 February in Toronto,
Canada, as Ephraim Owen
Goldberg
1947 Moves to California
1954 Bachelor of Architecture, University of Southern California,
followed by course of study in city
planning at the Graduate School
of Design, Harvard University
1961 Gehry moves to Paris with his
family for a year
1962 Founds his own architectural
office in Los Angeles
1972 "Easy Edges," furniture range in
corrugated board
1978 Gehry House in Santa Monica,
California, USA
1979 Founding of Gehry & Krueger Inc.
1982–84 California Aerospace
Museum, Los Angeles, USA
1986–89 Fishdance Restaurant, Kobe,
Japan
1989 Awarded the Pritzker Price
1992 Praemium Imperiale of the Japan
Art Association
1993–97 Guggenheim Museum,
Bilbao, Spain
1995 "Dancing House" (Ginger and
Fred), Prague, Czech Republic
1999 Gold Medal of the American
Institute of Architects
2000 DG Bank, Berlin, Germany
2002 Gehry Partners LLP founded
2003 Walt Disney Concert Hall, Los
Angeles, USA
2005 *Sketches of Frank Gehry,* documentary film by Sydney Pollack
2008 Museum of Tolerance, Jerusalem,
Israel

It ensured the revival of an entire city: Gehry's Guggenheim Museum for Bilbao

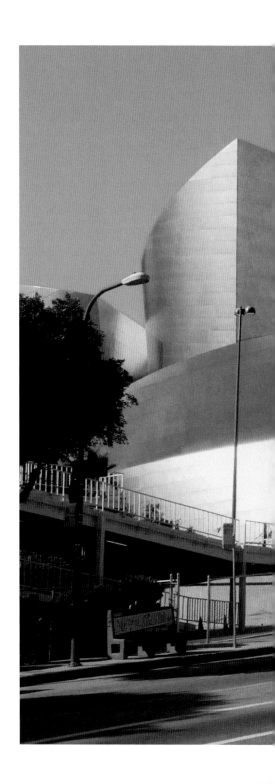

above
The courage to experiment: detail
of the Guggenheim Museum

right
The Walt Disney Concert Hall in
Los Angeles, built 1989–2004

1887–1889 Construction of
the Eiffel Tower in Paris

1914–1918 First World war

1883 First petrol-driven automobile,
Gottlieb Daimler and Carl Benz

1901 * Alberto Giacometti, Swiss
painter and sculptor, born

1922 Benito Mussolini becomes
prime minister of Italy

1886 Statue of Liberty, New York

1910 Futurist Manifesto, Italy

1929 Start of the
Great
Depression

1840–1895 REVIVALISM   **1895–1910 ART NOUVEAU   MODERNISM 1910–1980**

| 1850 | 1855 | 1860 | 1865 | 1870 | 1875 | 1880 | 1885 | 1890 | 1895 | 1900 | 1905 | 1910 | 1915 | 1920 | 1925 | 1930 | 1935 |

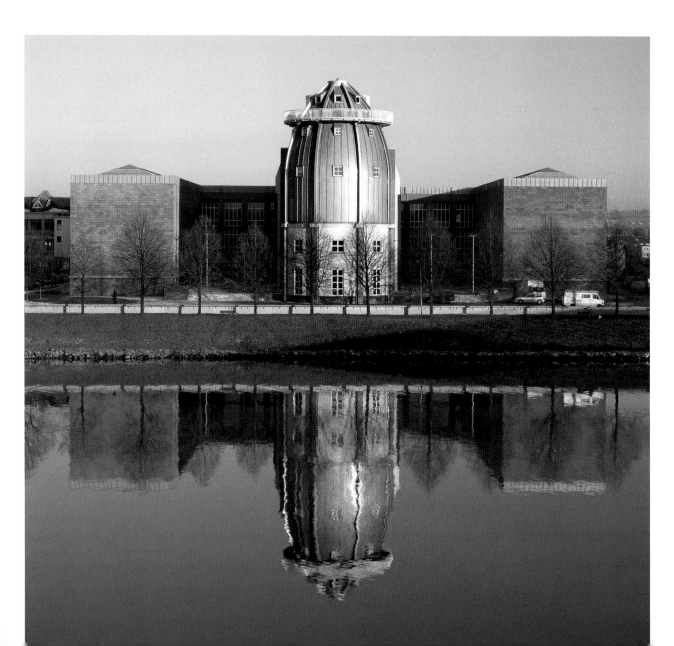

MARIO BOTTA, SWISS ARCHITECT

1946 First meeting of the United Nations   **1960** John F. Kennedy becomes   **1990** German reunification
US president
1939–1945 Second World War   **1950** India forms a republic   **1986** Chernobyl nuclear   **2001** September 11 attacks
reactor disaster
1943 The new government of Italy   **1955** Warsaw Pact   **1969** Neil Armstrong is the first person to set foot on the Moon   **1993** The Maastricht Treaty takes effect, for-
sides with the Allies and declares war on Germany   mally establishing the European Union
1910–1980 MODERNISM   POST-MODERNISM FROM 1980

1940   1945   1950   1955   1960   1965   1970   1975   1980   1985   1990   1995   2000   2005   2010   2015   2020   2025

ALDO ROSSI

"For me architecture is a whole, and I adopt good things wherever I find them." Aldo Rossi saw architecture not only from the viewpoint of the architect, but also from that of the theorist, the writer, and the artist. His drawings and paintings betoken a poetic perception of architecturally constructed worlds. A critic wrote that Rossi was "a poet who happens to be an architect."

Rossi combined universal forms and pastel colors in his characteristic compositions, whether in art or buildings. Through their use of space, both are reminiscent of the backdrops to be seen, for example, in the paintings of Giorgio de Chirico. Rossi was also a designer, and many furnishing accessories much in demand today are derived from his designs.

After completing his studies, he began his career working on an architectural magazine. All his life he made statements in writing on the theoretical problems of architecture, and as a lecturer he taught the Rationalism he practiced. As a 35-year-old he had already set out his principles in his most important book, *The Architecture of the City.* His theoretical ambition was not a modest one: the memory of place and regional traditions are the principles on which the architectural design should be based. The forms of historic buildings are classified in types. These form the artistic forms of expression of architecture, while questions of function are important but secondary. "What I reject is merely the naive concept of functionalism according to which functions determine form, and thus unequivocally determine urban planning and architecture." Rossi categorically rejected the famous slogan "form follows function." His view was rather that it was the continuity of the city that needed to be preserved. Thus a building, depending on its era, could alter its function, but not its historically determined image. New buildings should be adapted to the local forms of the past.

The identity of a building thus arises from its time, and only a building method linked to history is able to create identity. It was Rossi's wish to supply buildings with form from the fund of the collective memory—a poetic idea, whose artistic ambition must be measured by the reality of the use of his buildings.

One of his early buildings is the cemetery of San Cataldo in Modena. In the middle of the geometrically designed site stands a cube, whose many little square wall openings arranged in grid form find no correspondence in the interior, and thus create a "lifeless" effect, which is precisely what was intended. This cemetery built on the principle of the square succeeds, in accordance with Rossi's theory, in expressing meaning through primary forms or types of architecture.

The repertoire of forms from which Aldo Rossi drew is related to the theater and its stage sets. For him the city was the true theater of life, and architecture the backdrop. Significantly, he built a floating theater for the Venice Biennale of 1979; his strangely timeless structure, giving the effect of stage décor, was understood as homage to an old Venetian tradition. It was recreated in 2004 on the occasion of an exhibition in Genoa.

Two years before his death, the Bonnefanten Museum in Maastricht was opened. This redbrick building is E-shaped, with in its center a zinc-covered, rocket-shaped tower as an eye-catcher and signature feature of the museum. The unpretentious forms in the interior, together with an abundance of daylight and wood, ensure a friendly atmosphere.

Friendly and imaginative, too, were the many drawings created in the course of time by this versatile architect and artist—and it is from them that the cities of his dreams were created.

1931 Born 3 May, in Milan, Italy
1959 Receives his diploma from the Politecnico di Milano
1955–64 Works on the magazine *Casabella-Continuità*
FROM 1963 Serves his apprenticeship, from 1972 at the Federal Technical College, Zurich
1966 Publishes *The Architecture of the City*
1971–78 Cemetery of San Cataldo, Modena
1970 Housing estates at Gallaratese near Milan
1979 Floating Teatro del Mondo for the Venice Biennale
1988 Lighthouse Theater, Toronto
1990–94 Bonnefanten Museum, Maastricht
1990 Awarded the Pritzker Prize
1991–93 Extension of Linate Airport, Milan
1997 Dies 4 September, in Milan

Brick building with an eye-catching tower: Rossi's Bonnefanten Museum in Maastricht

1883 First petrol-driven automobile, Gottlieb Daimler and Carl Benz

1901 Queen Victoria of Britain dies

1914–1918 First World war

1929 Start of the Great Depression

1853–1856 Crimean War

1874 * Winston Churchill, British statesman, born

1886 Statue of Liberty, New York

1907 *Les Demoiselles d'Avignon,* Pablo Picasso

1922 * Lucian Freud, British painter, born

1840–1895 REVIVALISM   **1895–1910 ART NOUVEAU**   **MODERNISM 1910–1980**

| 1850 | 1855 | 1860 | 1865 | 1870 | 1875 | 1880 | 1885 | 1890 | 1895 | 1900 | 1905 | 1910 | 1915 | 1920 | 1925 | 1930 | 1935 |

The Headquarters of Lloyd's of London, completed 1986

1946 First meeting of the United Nations 1969 Neil Armstrong is the first person to set foot on the Moon 1990 German reunification
1955 Warsaw Pact 1979 Margaret Thatcher becomes 1986 Chernobyl nuclear
1939–1945 Second World War Prime minister of Great Britain reactor disaster
1960 John F. Kennedy wins the United 1987 The Single European Act is 2001 September 11 attacks
States presidential election passed by the European Union

1910–1980 MODERNISM POST-MODERNISM FROM 1980

1940 1945 1950 1955 1960 1965 1970 1975 1980 1985 1990 1995 2000 2005 2010 2015 2020 2025

RICHARD ROGERS

For more than 30 years, what is probably Richard Rogers' most famous building, in the center of Paris, has unfailingly continued to draw the crowds: the Centre Pompidou, the culture machine of the 1970s, designed and built by him together with his friend Renzo Piano.

They had the ground breaking idea of making the structure, until then always covered up, as well as functional elements of the interior, in bright colors, into the actual theme of the façade, and thus of the architecture. This concept allowed the interior spaces an unprecedented flexibility. The forecourt, today used as a social meeting point for tourists, entertainers, and passers-by, had been deliberately integrated into the plans, and the concept of a cultural structure that would be easily and playfully accessible to the general public took off.

Although critics from conservative circles feared that it would be a blight on the historic center of the French capital, this monument rapidly became one of the most popular venues and attractions in Paris. Of course, this milestone of museum history was not the end of the story. Richard Rogers and his firm have created many memorable buildings, chiefly in Europe. Among these is the Millennium Dome in Greenwich, London, created for the celebration of this landmark in time, a gigantic tent structure with 12 towers rising up to the sky like birthday candles on a cake.

Visible construction elements, mechanically playful forms, these are the characteristic components of the work of Richard Rogers. The building is turned inside out, making the functions of the architectural elements clearly recognizable.

Of the many projects of Richard Rogers, to whom, on the occasion of the 30th birthday of the building, an exhibition was dedicated in 2007 in the Centre Pompidou, the headquarters of Lloyd's in London is one of the most emblematic buildings. In the heart of the City, London's financial district, here as in the Centre Pompidou, the functional elements (such as lifts and cables) are located outside and in special tower annexes, in order to gain maximum space inside. The extension of the spaces was to remain flexible. The façade conveys the impression of a large mechanism, which matches perfectly with function of the building—the financial machine.

In recent years, Rogers has turned more and more to considerations of the durability of the building and to the conservation of the environment. Each of his projects is focused on these qualities. The building designed by Rogers in 1998 for the Welsh Assembly and occupied since 2005, for example, is very economical in its energy use when compared to traditional buildings. The appearance of the building stands for openness, democracy and participation. A project not necessarily compatible with Rogers' political statements is One Hyde Park. In the center of London four residential towers for the super-rich have been created, whose prices, even before the completion of the building, have broken all world records. The architecture makes full use of the contemporary technological potential for the conservation of energy and materials. Made of weathered red steel and glass, this residential complex hit the headlines with its further ultimate technological refinements, such as bulletproof walls and windows, private lifts, 24-hour hotel service, and the like. In the words of an estate agent, "One Hyde Park is a new residential scheme whose beauty, luxury and prestige will place it in a class of its own."

In fact, Rogers' interest is in social improvement. He sits in the House of Lords on behalf of the Labour Party, and in his office, Rogers Stirk Harbour & Partners, value is placed on the encouragement of new blood, a commitment to charitable work, and social justice. With more than 180 staff members, the salary of the best-paid architect in the enterprise is thus linked to that of the lowest-paid.

Rogers is optimistic about his central preoccupation, the question of the development of cities. They "will no longer be zoned as today in isolated one-activity ghettos; rather they will resemble the more richly layered cities of the past. Living, work, shopping, learning, and leisure will overlap and be housed in continuous, varied and changing structures."

1933 Born 23 July, in Florence, Italy
1954–59 Studies at the Architectural Association School in London
1961 Receives his diploma in architecture from Yale, then works at Skidmore, Owings & Merrill (SOM)
1963–67 Sets up the joint architectural practice Team 4 Architects with his first wife Su Rogers, Norman Foster, and Foster's future wife, Wendy Cheesman
1971 Founds the office of Piano & Rogers
1971–77 Centre Pompidou, Paris, with Renzo Piano
1977 Founds his own firm, now Rogers, Stirk, Harbour & Partners
1978–86 Lloyd's headquarters in London
1985 Awarded RIBA (Royal Institute of British Architects) Gold Medal
1989–95 European Court of Human Rights, Strasbourg
1993–99 Daimler-Chrysler Building, Potsdamer Platz, Berlin
1998–2005 Courthouse, Antwerp
1999/2000 Millennium Dome, London
2005 Barajas International Airport, Madrid
2007 Awarded the Pritzker Prize

1886 Statue of Liberty, New York

1883 First petrol-driven automobile,
Gottlieb Daimler and Carl Benz

1891 End of the Indian Wars in the USA

1914–1918 First World war

1928 * Andy Warhol,
American artist
born

1929 Start of the
Great
Depression

1840–1895 REVIVALISM   1895–1910 ART NOUVEAU   MODERNISM 1910–1980

| 1850 | 1855 | 1860 | 1865 | 1870 | 1875 | 1880 | 1885 | 1890 | 1895 | 1900 | 1905 | 1910 | 1915 | 1920 | 1925 | 1930 | 1935 |

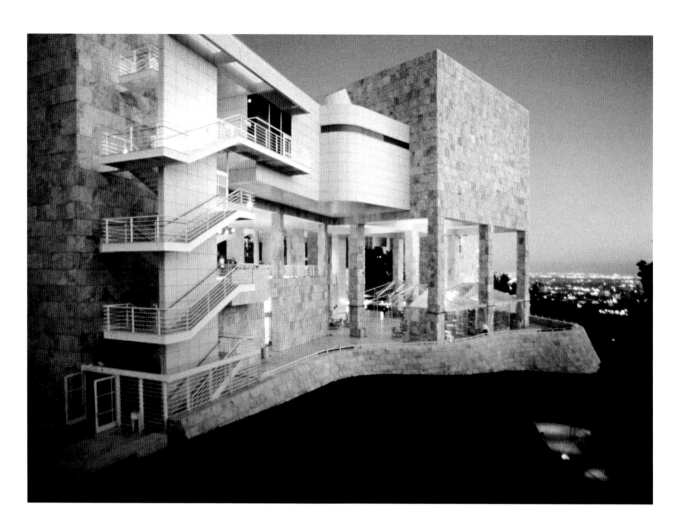

STEVEN HOLL, AMERICAN ARCHITECT   1967 Six-Day War in the Middle East

Guernica, Pablo Picasso   1950 India forms a republic   1963 John F. Kennedy assassination in Dallas, Texas   1990 German reunification

1939–1945 Second World War   1969 Neil Armstrong is the   1986 Chernobyl nuclear   2001 September 11 attacks
1948 United Nations General Assembly adopts   first person to set foot on   reactor disaster   2003 Third Gulf War (US invasion of Iraq)
Universal Declaration of Human Rights   the Moon

1910–1980 MODERNISM   POST-MODERNISM FROM 1980

1940   1945   1950   1955   1960   1965   1970   1975   1980   1985   1990   1995   2000   2005   2010   2015   2020   2025

RICHARD MEIER

A documentary film about the architect Richard Meier proclaims him "The Magician of Light," and although he is not a magician but an architect, the title is illuminating in the truest sense of the word.

As early as the 1960s, white villas against a blue American sky have gone into architectural history as icons of Meier's work. Clear geometrical forms, combined with intelligently arranged window areas, soon ensured his popularity as an architect.

His initial fame in the United States was due to his family houses with their characteristic white façades and light-flooded interiors. His declared favorite color is white, and only in exceptional cases does he deviate from it. It allows him, by means of skilful handling of light through generous openings in the walls, to reproduce daylight situations in the interior, and thus to create changing atmospheres. Meier himself says that "for me, white is the most wonderful color because within it you can see all the colors of the rainbow. For me, in fact, it is the color which in natural light, reflects and intensifies the perception of all of the shades of the rainbow, the colors which are constantly changing in nature, for the whiteness of white is never just white; it is almost always transformed by light and that which is changing; the sky, the clouds, the sun and the moon."

This is how he describes the origins of his aesthetic: "We are all affected by Le Corbusier, Frank Lloyd Wright, Alvar Aalto, and Mies van der Rohe. But no less than Bramante, Borromini and Bernini. Architecture is a tradition, a long continuum. Whether we break with tradition or enhance it, we are still connected to that past. We evolve."

Since his beginnings, Meier has remained true to his Bauhaus-inspired style.

He has brought his development and that of his firm successfully through the last 40 years, and is also represented in Europe by a large number of his projects. His unornamented, lucid buildings are particularly popular for museum architecture.

His first museum building was the Museum für Angewandte Kunst in Frankfurt, built in 1985. Proportionally adapted to the existing villa, built around 1800, his three white interlinked cubes are incorporated into the park area of the Museum Mile on the Schaumainkai. The White Cube is a principle of exhibiting, in which the architecture of the showroom is reduced to the pure white, ideally square space in order not to interfere with the perception of the artworks. With Meier, this principle of the interior space is in a sense relocated to the exterior; his unobtrusive and elegant forms adapt themselves to the environment.

Further well-known museum buildings are the Museum for Contemporary Art (Museu d'Art Contemporani–MACBA) in Barcelona and the prestigious complex of the J. Paul Getty Center near Los Angeles, opened in 1997. On the hill lie the six buildings, linked together below ground, forming a campus that serves the museum and research institute as well as the reception of visitors. Meier's trademark white is here exceptionally replaced by the color of the natural stone.

A self-confessed New Yorker, in 2002 Meier was able to set his seal on the city skyline in the form of two apartment towers with a view of the Hudson river—luxury living space with glamorous inhabitants, maliciously described by some as goldfish in their bowl. The two towers rise high above their neighbors, and are constructed neither of the brick typical of this part of New York, nor with an exclusively glass façade. Here glass is framed by white aluminum, placing Meier's emphasis on the urban image.

Despite the range of very different buildings he has created, his designs have characteristic features that make them recognized worldwide, notably: clear and elegant lines, the use of white, interiors flooded with light, and proportions adapted to a specific environment.

1934 Born 12 October, in Newark, New Jersey
1952 Receives his diploma from Cornell University
1960 Works with SOM (Skidmore Owings & Merrill)
1960–63 Works with Marcel Breuer
1963 Founds his own office
1969 Exhibition *The New York Five* (with John Hejduk, Michael Graves, Peter Eisenman, and Charles Gwathmey)
1979–85 Museum für Angewandte Kunst, Frankfurt, Germany
1984 Awarded the Pritzker Prize
1984–97 The Getty Centre, Los Angeles
1987–95 Museum for Contemporary Art, MACBA, Barcelona, Spain
1989 Awarded the RIBA (Royal Institute of British Architects) Gold Medal
2004 Frieder Burda Collection Museum, Baden-Baden

With a view across the sea of lights: the J. Paul Getty Center near Los Angeles

JAMES STIRLING, BRITISH ARCHITECT

RICHARD ROGERS, BRITISH ARCHITECT

1883 First petrol-driven automobile,
Gottlieb Daimler and Carl Benz

1901 Queen Victoria of Britain dies

1853–1856 Crimean War

1874 * Winston Churchill,
British statesman, born

1907 *Les Demoiselles d'Avignon*,
Pablo Picasso

1922 * Lucian Freud, British
painter, born

1886 Statue of Liberty, New York

1914–1918 First World war

1840–1895 REVIVALISM   **1895–1910 ART NOUVEAU**   **MODERNISM 1910–1980**

1850   1855   1860   1865   1870   1875   1880   1885   1890   1895   1900   1905   1910   1915   1920   1925   1930   1935

Known as the "Gherkin" –
the headquarters of the Swiss
Re insurance company

1939–1945 Second World War   1955 Warsaw Pact
1946 First meeting
of the United Nations
1950 India becomes
a republic
1960 John F. Kennedy becomes
president of the US

1986 Chernobyl nuclear reactor disaster
1981 First flight of the space-shuttle Columbia
1979 Margaret Thatcher becomes
Prime minister of Great Britain
2001 September 11 attacks
2003 Third Gulf War (US invasion of Iraq)

1910–1980 MODERNISM   POST-MODERNISM FROM 1980

1940   1945   1950   1955   1960   1965   1970   1975   1980   1985   1990   1995   2000   2005   2010   2015   2020   2025

NORMAN FOSTER

Buildings from the Hong Kong and Shanghai Bank high-rise in Hong Kong and the Reichstag building in Berlin to the Millau viaduct in France, two and a half kilometers long, testify to Norman Foster's characteristic combination of inventive design, superb engineering, and ecological concerns.

At the age of 32, Foster, who grew up in Manchester, founded his own architectural firm, which today employs more than 1,200 staff in 22 offices worldwide. A special form of organization enables Foster to remain to the greatest possible extent informed about his many building projects.

The Sainsbury Centre for Visual Arts in Norwich, England, which apart from exhibition galleries also accommodates study and eating areas, has also contributed to his fame—a large-scale, open building, whose modular construction from ready-made parts is made visible by the supporting framework. A great deal of natural light is able to enter by day, and by night the artificial lighting gives the campus a special atmosphere.

Also in the cultural area, this time in France, is the Carré d'Art in Nîmes, completed in 1993. This modern building adopts the proportions of the Roman palace opposite, and is among the museum attractions that have altered the life of a city.

In London, apart from the daring structure of the Millennium Bridge and the canopy and redesign of the British Museum, it is certainly the high-rise building for the insurance company Swiss Re that has aroused the greatest public interest (and has also been a bone of contention). On the Swiss Re tower, which has been nicknamed the "Gherkin" by Londoners, and about whose construction a film has even been made, a journalist wrote: "If at least one scene of the next James Bond film is not set here, I'll eat my hat."

And Foster's buildings really are high tech, not to be outdone by anything that an inventor for an intelligence service could have devised. Even his early projects caused surprise at the economical and energy-saving way they were built, as well as the fact that they were sometimes even completed ahead of schedule.

Foster's enthusiasm and his ambition to create ever taller, larger, and more spectacular buildings have naturally also led him into the great contemporary centers of building such as Abu Dhabi, where his enterprises at the present time include projects such as the Aldar Central Market and the Masdar Development. Durability is a matter of great importance in futuristic projects, and so Masdar is an ecologically ambitions project, a green city in the middle of the desert, which is to use only half of the energy usually required. Here 40,000 individuals are to be able to live. For Foster this project represents an important symbol, intended to arouse hope of a better future—a future that he has foreshadowed with his buildings and ideas.

1935 Born in Manchester, England
1961 Receives a diploma from the Manchester University School of Architecture and City Planning, and a scholarship to Yale School of Architecture
1967 Founds Foster Associates, now Foster + Partners
1974–78 Sainsbury Centre for Visual Arts, Norwich, England
1979–85 Hong Kong and Shanghai Bank, Hong Kong
1983 Awarded the RIBA (Royal Institute of British Architects) Gold Medal
1984–92 Carré d'Art, Nîmes, France
1985–92 Sackler Art Gallery, Royal Academy of Arts, London
1987 Stansted Airport, England
1991–97 Commerzbank, Frankfurt
1992–99 Rebuilding of Reichstag/ German Bundestag, Berlin
1993–2004 Millau Viaduct, France
1994–2000 The Great Court, British Museum, London
1996–2000 Millennium Bridge, London
1999 Awarded the Pritzker Prize
2003–08 Beijing Airport, Peking
2004 Swiss Re tower ("Gherkin"), London

The head office of the Hong Kong and Shanghai Banking Corporation (HSBC Tower) in Hong Kong

1872 *Impression, Sunrise*, Claude Monet

1881 * Pablo Picasso, Spanish artist, born

1866 * Wassily Kandinsky, Russian painter, born

1871 Foundation of the German Empire

1929 Start of the Great Depression

1914–1918 First World war

1840–1895 REVIVALISM   1895–1910 ART NOUVEAU   MODERNISM 1910–1980

| 1850 | 1855 | 1860 | 1865 | 1870 | 1875 | 1880 | 1885 | 1890 | 1895 | 1900 | 1905 | 1910 | 1915 | 1920 | 1925 | 1930 | 1935 |

above
View of the Berlin Hauptbahnhof

below
A city comes into being: Lingang near Shanghai is
to create space for 800,000 people

1939–1945 Second World War   1961 Berlin Wall erected
1944 Allied troops land on the beaches   1963 John F. Kennedy assassination in Dallas, Texas   1990 German reunification
of Normandy during D-Day
1969 Neil Armstrong is the first person to set foot on the Moon   2001 September 11 attacks
1949 Democratic Republic of Germany   1972 Summer Olympics take place in Munich
DDR established officially
1910–1980 MODERNISM   POST-MODERNISM FROM 1980

1940   1945   1950   1955   1960   1965   1970   1975   1980   1985   1990   1995   2000   2005   2010   2015   2020   2025

GMP (VON GERKAN, MARG UND PARTNER)

The building of the new main railway station in Berlin was awaited with excitement. The site itself was a curiosity: while building work went ahead, a viewing platform continually drew masses of curious observers. This building is among the most important to have been created in Germany in recent years, and not only in terms of transport technology.

Admittedly its appearance does not correspond in all respects to the original design by von Gerkan, Marg und Partner, and the media have reported on the legal disputes between the client, Deutsche Bahn, and the architect Meinhard von Gerkan, whose copyright was been injured by them. In the meantime, not only has the dispute been settled, but also the building has been completed.

Two towers out of a steel supporting structure are linked by a barrel roof lying between them, glazed like the façades, with the outer, identically arched, platform roofs running at right angles to it. In an allusion to the tradition of railway stations with light-filled halls of steel and glass, this building was ennobled before its completion with the title "Cathedral of Mobility." A symbolic structure, in which railway tracks run crosswise from all points of the compass meet, and where the passenger changing trains has a choice of 80 shops. Above the enormous glass roof of the station, solar energy is produced in exemplary fashion.

Forty years ago, Meinhard von Gerkan and his fellow-student Volkwin Marg founded an architectural firm that today operates worldwide, with more than 300 staff. This makes it one of the largest in Germany. They have already built more than 230 buildings, and are diligently continuing to build on a large number of sites all over the world, particularly in China.

gmp became well known for building the geometrically constructed, car-friendly Tegel Airport in Berlin of 1975; airports in Stuttgart and Hamburg followed. Huge structures such as these airports, trade fair sites, stadiums and theaters (and more recently, even whole cities) are the preferred field of activity of this firm.

gmp's architects see themselves as artists in building. They want to combine the traditions of architecture with the possibilities of modern construction methods. Technology, art, and architecture should become one; a building method not adapted to the place, or too eccentric in form, is not their style. Volkwin Marg explains how essential it is for him to bring technology and art together into a new synthesis, the art of building: "I don't see that bridging the gulf between technology and art is a problem. This is why I am irritated by the brazenness of seemingly wise gurus who flirt with chaos and break historically evolved tectonic expressions into fractals, or blow them up to blobs based on incoherent philosophies."

gmp's buildings are technologically very ambitious, and are mostly executed within the given time frame and budget. In China, too, the firm has had a sweeping success. There, apart from many public buildings, gmp are building nothing less than a whole city. A project of superlatives—the satellite city of Lingang, near Shanghai, which is to provide living space for 800,000 individuals. "The city of Alexandria, one of the seven wonders of the world, was godfather to the design; the quality of life close to water is a reference to Hamburg." A statement such as this, between high-flying ambition and a solidly down-to-earth attitude, between idealism and a sense of reality, is characteristic of the gmp enterprise and its architectural work.

MEINHARD VON GERKAN
1935 Born 3 January, in Riga, Latvia
1964 Receives his diploma from the Technical University of Braunschweig
FROM 1972 Active as a teacher and in various organizations

VOLKWIN MARG
1936 Born 15 January, in Königsberg, East Prussia (now Kaliningrad, Russia)
1964 Receives his diploma from the Technical University of Braunschweig
FROM 1972 Active as a teacher and in various organizations
1979–83 President of the BDA (Association of German Architects)

1965 The two architects found a firm together
1970–75 Tegel Airport, Berlin
1993–95 New Trade Fair building, Leipzig
1999–2001 New Tempodrom, Berlin
1996–2006 Main railway station, Berlin
FROM 1998 Increasingly active in China

1883 First petrol-driven automobile,
Gottlieb Daimler and Carl Benz

1891 End of the Indian Wars in the USA

1886 Statue of Liberty, New York

1907 *Les Demoiselles d'Avignon*, Pablo Picasso

1914–1918 First World war

1928 * Andy Warhol,
American artist,

1929 Start of the Gre
Depression

1931 Empire State Bu
ing the highest
building in the v

1840–1895 REVIVALISM   1895–1910 ART NOUVEAU   MODERNISM 1910–1980

| 1850 | 1855 | 1860 | 1865 | 1870 | 1875 | 1880 | 1885 | 1890 | 1895 | 1900 | 1905 | 1910 | 1915 | 1920 | 1925 | 1930 | 1935 |

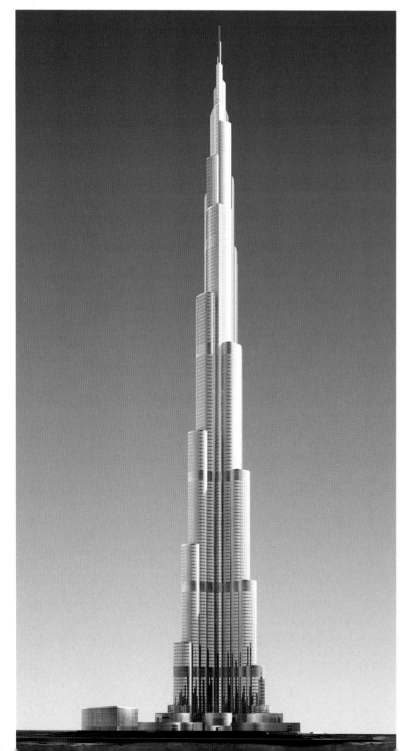

A building of superlatives: the skyscraper Burj Dubai,
the tallest building in the world

DANIEL LIBESKIND, AMERICAN ARCHITECT   **1969** Neil Armstrong is the first person to set foot on the Moon   **2001** September 11 attacks

1948 United Nations Gen-   **1963** Assassination of John F. Kennedy   **1990** German reunification **2003** Third Gulf War (US invasion of Iraq)
eral Assembly adopts   **1967** Six-Day War in the Middle East   **1986** Chernobyl nuclear reactor disaster
1939–1945 Second   Universal Declaration **1959** Frank Lloyd Wright's Guggenheim   **1997** Frank O. Gehry's Guggenheim
World War   of Human Rights   Museum is completed   Museum Bilbao is completed
1910–1980 MODERNISM   POST-MODERNISM FROM 1980

1940   1945   1950   1955   1960   1965   1970   1975   1980   1985   1990   1995   2000   2005   2010   2015   2020   2025

SOM (SKIDMORE, OWINGS & MERRILL LLP)

How can one characterize Skidmore, Owings & Merrill? The firm, founded in 1936, is an anomaly—a design firm that gives technical excellence and business responsibility equal weight with design excellence; a design firm that has outlasted its original founders for four generations of partners; a design firm that is not centered on a single designer or personality but rather a collective enterprise that values collective competence.

SOM is also a business that employs nearly 1,500 architects, engineers, interior designers and other staff, who, together, are capable of dealing with all the stages of planning in projects of all kinds throughout the world. Even in its beginnings, the firm focused on highly complex, large and very public commissions. What is special about it is its collective nature, in which individuals remain largely anonymous. Instead of individual fame, emphasis is placed on systematic internal collaboration in design, planning, and execution. Since its foundation, the firm has handled more than 10,000 projects.

The avant-garde character of SOM, accordingly, lies in its functional and formal qualities and its technological innovations, such as the early use of computers in the most varied processes, which has been systematically developed within the company (the firm developed a software for Building Information Modeling, the first of its kind, in the early 1980s). Engineering skill and a definitively rational mode of operation make SOM, among other things, the epitome of technologically impeccable skyscraper construction. But beyond this, the firm also offers expertise in the areas of urban planning and interior architecture. In its more than 70-year history, SOM has completed projects of just about every conceivable type, in countries around the world.

Among the best-known building by Skidmore, Owings & Merrill is the Sears Tower, completed in Chicago in 1974. At 463 meters, it was at that time the tallest building in the world. It followed the tradition, founded in Chicago in the 19th century, of high-rise buildings based on a steel skeleton structure, and was emblematic, as skyscrapers still are today, of prosperity, optimism, and strength. Among architectural firms in the second half of the 20th century, the abbreviation SOM was shorthand for a firm specializing in towers of this kind.

It was SOM's technical know-how that brought it the commission to build the new "Freedom Tower" on the site of the World Trade Center, destroyed in 2001—a project highly charged with symbolism, which in addition to great architectural challenges also needed to satisfy content-related demands. These demands are summed up as follows by SOM: "While the memorial, carved out of the earth, speaks of the past and of remembrance, Freedom Tower speaks about the future and hope as it rises into the sky." The design and building of the new tower in Manhattan are accompanied by the interest of an international public.

In Dubai, plans were made for a new "tallest skyscraper in the world," the Burj Dubai. Meanwhile, however, it was announced that another skyscraper, the Al Burj, would tower over it. In any case it is one of the tallest buildings ever built. Its structure tapers upwards in a staggered formation in order to minimize the effect of wind. The ambitious plans of the rulers of the Arab Emirates demanded that the whole world should be visible from the record heights of the Burj Dubai. What was meant were the 300 artificial islands in the bay of Dubai, which are laid out in the form of a world map. A truly Babylonian project—to reach for the sky and look down upon the world. SOM's technology makes it possible.

Founded in 1936 by
Louis Skidmore (1897–1962)
Nathaniel Owings (1903–1984)
from 1939 with John Merrill (1896–1975)
www.som.com

left
On a clear day, the observation platform
of the Sears Tower in Chicago allows a
view of four federal states of the USA

above
A new beginning for Ground Zero:
the Freedom Tower in New York

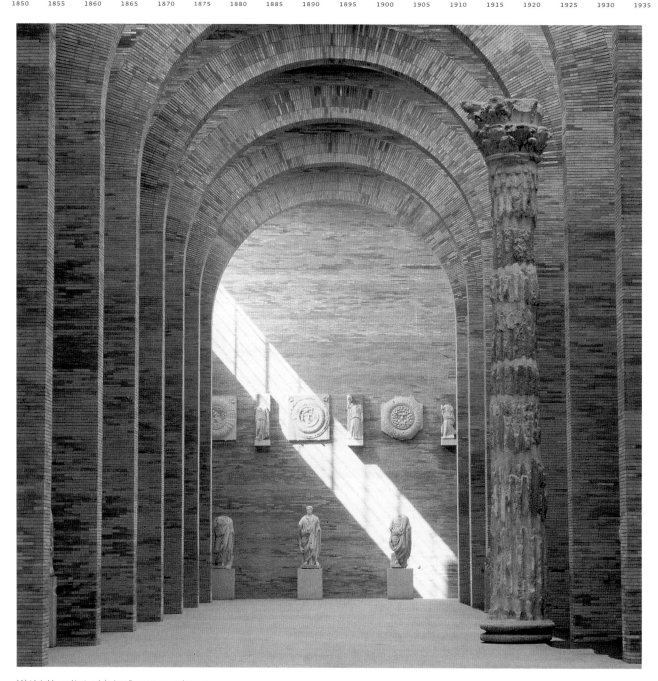

ANTONI GAUDÍ, SPANISH ARCHITECT

JOAN MIRÓ, SPANISH ARTIST

1871 Foundation of the German Empire

1904 * Salvador Dalí, Spanish artist, born

1866 * Wassily Kandinsky, Russian painter, born

1890 Dutch painter Vincent van Gogh dies

1914–1918 First World war

1929 Start of the Great Depression

1840–1895 REVIVALISM   **1895–1910 ART NOUVEAU**   **MODERNISM 1910–1980**

1850 1855 1860 1865 1870 1875 1880 1885 1890 1895 1900 1905 1910 1915 1920 1925 1930 1935

Mérida's Museo Nacional de Arte Romano, opened in 1986

right page
For the artist Joan Miró's foundation, his former home and
studio were redesigned

–1939 Spanish Civil War

1939–1945 Second World War

1944 Allied troops land on the beaches of Normandy during D-Day

1946 First meeting of the United Nations

1961 Berlin Wall erected

1963 John F. Kennedy assassination in Dallas, Texas

1969 Neil Armstrong is the first person to set foot on the Moon

1972 Summer Olympics take place in Munich

1975 Dictator of Spain Franco dies

1990 German reunification

2001 September 11 attacks

1910–1980 MODERNISM   POST-MODERNISM FROM 1980

1940 1945 1950 1955 1960 1965 1970 1975 1980 1985 1990 1995 2000 2005 2010 2015 2020 2025

RAFAEL MONEO

The Spanish architect Rafael Moneo is equally at home on building sites and in lecture halls. His creative career is divided between technology and texts, buildings and books.

The Museum of Roman Art in Merida, opened in 1986, is one of his most celebrated buildings. The city has an important Roman past, which was to be made accessible again for visitors. Situated directly next to an excavation site, the building's form and dimensions have been adapted to the historic architecture. By means of solid walls and round arches, it effectively stages an appeerence recalling the Roman Empire, in which remains of buildings and archaeological objects are shown to full advantage. It is not a question here of making a copy of historical buildings, but rather of the intelligent incorporation of forms from the past into a contemporary structure.

Another building created only a short time later is presented quite differently. In the middle of a hill in Palma de Mallorca, on which rapid and intensive building work has been carried out, Moneo has built a veritable fortress between the former studio and private residence of the artist Joan Miró. The foundation bearing the name of the artist and his wife is accommodated in an asymmetrically serrated building, which seems to defend itself against its neighbors. Alabaster shades are applied to the windows. The sea is no longer visible from this spot on account of the dominant buildings round about, but the architect has made up for this by building a swimming pool on the roof. In these rooms, screened off from the noisy outside world, the beach-weary visitor can now admire the art of Joan Miró in a tranquil setting.

The presentation of art is also important at the other end of Europe: Rafael Moneo was also commissioned to build the Museum of Modern Art and Architecture in Stockholm. As a young architect he had already worked in the office of Jørn Utzon, the creator of Sydney Opera House, and was therefore able to boast some experience in Nordic countries. Composed of several building units adapted in their proportions to their surroundings, the museum stands in immediate proximity to water, on an island in the harbor. Its most striking feature are the lanterns, in the form of glass cubes, on the roof hoods, through which light enters the exhibition spaces from above.

After the success of his Stockholm museum, Moneo received the prestigious task of enlarging the Prado in Madrid. He has doubled the area of the museum. Next to the venerable 18th-century art museum, the extension building is a red-brick cube standing on a granite base, with a columned façade, which fits unpretentiously, but with a character all of its own, into the urban environment. Inside, the cloister, formerly in a ruined state, rises into new life, adding a mystical element to the new structure. The newly gained spaces are primarily devoted to special exhibitions, various visitor areas and administrative offices for the museum staff.

Rafael Moneo stresses the importance of the specific location for architecture: "The shadow of anywhere is haunting our world today ... architecture claims the site from anywhere ... Architecture is engendered upon it ... The site is where architecture is. It can't be anywhere."

As a professor, Moneo teaches this principle in theoretical terms; as an architect, he proves it in practice.

1937 Born José Rafael Moneo Vallés, 9 May, in Tudela, Spain

1961 Receives his diploma in architecture from the Escuela Tecnica Superior de Arquitectura de Madrid

1961–62 Works with Jørn Utzon (architect of Sydney Opera House) in Denmark

1965 Founds his own firm in Madrid

1970–80 Teaches at the University of Barcelona

FROM 1976 Teaches in the USA

1980–84 Teaches at the Escuela Tecnica Superior de Arquitectura de Madrid

1984–92 Atocha Railway Station, Madrid

1985–90 Serves as head of the architecture faculty at Harvard University

1980–86 National Museum of Roman Art, Merida, Spain

1987–92 Pilar and Joan Miró Foundation, Palma de Mallorca

1989–92 Thyssen-Bornemisza Museum/ redesign of the Villahermosa Palace, Madrid

1990 Resumes work at his architectural office, retaining his post as professor

1991–98 Museum of Modern Art and Architecture, Stockholm, Sweden

1993–98 Hotel Hyatt and office buildings, Potsdamer Platz, Berlin

1996 Awarded the Pritzker Prize

1998–2007 Enlargement of the Prado Museum, Madrid

1887–1889 Construction of the Eiffel Tower in Paris

1883 First petrol-driven automobile,
Gottlieb Daimler and Carl Benz

1901 * Alberto Giacometti, Swiss
painter and sculptor, born

1922 Benito Mussolini becomes
prime minister of Italy

1886 Statue of Liberty,
New York

1910 Futurist Manifesto, Italy

1929 Start of the
Great
Depression

1914–1918 First World war

1840–1895 REVIVALISM   **1895–1910 ART NOUVEAU**   **MODERNISM 1910–1980**

| 1850 | 1855 | 1860 | 1865 | 1870 | 1875 | 1880 | 1885 | 1890 | 1895 | 1900 | 1905 | 1910 | 1915 | 1920 | 1925 | 1930 | 1935 |

1946 First meeting of the
United Nations

1939–1945 Second World War

1943 The new government of Italy sides with
the Allies and declares war on Germany

1960 John F. Kennedy becomes
president of the US

1955 Warsaw Pact

1981 First flight of the space-shuttle Columbia

1986 Chernobyl nuclear
reactor disaster

1973 First oil crisis

1990 German reunification

2001 September 11 attacks

1993 The Maastricht Treaty takes effect, formally
establishing the European Union

1910–1980 MODERNISM   POST-MODERNISM FROM 1980

1940   1945   1950   1955   1960   1965   1970   1975   1980   1985   1990   1995   2000   2005   2010   2015   2020   2025

RENZO PIANO

"An architect has the best job in the world, for on this little planet, where everything has already been discovered, the design of a project remains one of the greatest adventures still possible for us." Renzo Piano

Renzo Piano says of himself that he has no style. At least not a recognizable one, not a style which makes everyone think straight away, "Ah, a building by Renzo Piano": "I don't like the idea that you have, at the earliest stages, when you start to design, to put your own stamp on a building. For example, I love working with very light elements, transparency, and natural light. So when the building's finished, you recognize those elements in some way. But I think imposing your style may be actually very limiting, because you may end by simply imposing your style, instead of understanding the need of people."

Renzo Piano researches every location before he builds on it. This creative way of going about things has made him an architect in great demand, with commissions coming from all over the world. His business, the Renzo Piano Building Workshop, with offices in Genoa and Paris, employs about a hundred staff. Piano's preoccupation with the location and the precise purpose and ambition of the building to be executed allows the creative process, from sketches by way of models to the actual building, to become a process that he loves.

He explains this on the basis of his experiences in early childhood. As a small boy he often accompanied his father, a civil engineer, to building sites, and became enthusiastic about the development of a building, which appeared a magical process to him. One of his best-known and earliest buildings is the Centre Pompidou in Paris, designed and built together with Richard Rogers (see page 113). This cultural center is a favorite with the public in the middle of Paris. Piano, who lives and works quite nearby, was able to follow at close quarters the development of his cultural machine, designed—not without irony in the face of technology—like a colorful giant mechanical toy, and of the piazza in front of it.

His hobby, building his own sailing boats, allows him to carry out creative tests on new materials

that may later be useful to him in his architectural projects. Technical sophistication and solid craftsmanship definitely characterize Piano's buildings. His Kansai International Airport in Osaka had just been completed when a severe earthquake in Japan caused great damage—but his wave-shaped building was unscathed.

Soon after the turn of the millennium, Piano was positively inundated with commissions in New York. He built, for example, the New York Times Building, and was entrusted with the extensions of the Whitney Museum of Art, Columbia University, and the Morgan Library. His special interest in buildings intended to be accessible to a large public continues unabated.

Probably one of his most exciting projects in recent years is the Jean-Marie Tjibaou Cultural Center in Nouméa, New Caledonia. Here, in allusion to the local hut structure, ten buildings of wood with steel and glass have been erected in a wildlife park as a cultural center for the Kanak culture, creating a true skyline in the middle of the island state in the Pacific.

Piano writes with enthusiasm about his work: "An architect's profession is an adventurous enterprise: a profession between art and science, between invention and memory, between the audacity of modernity and true respect for tradition. The architect lives dangerously, out of necessity. He works with all sorts of materials, by which I mean not only concrete, wood and metal, but also history and geography, mathematics and science, anthropology and ecology, aesthetics and technology, climate and society. Every day he must pit himself against all these things."

1937 Born 14 September, in Genoa, Italy

1964 Receives his diploma in architecture from the Politecnico di Milano

1971 Founds the office of Piano & Rogers

1971–77 Centre Pompidou, Paris, with Richard Rogers

1977 Founds the studio Piano & Rice with Peter Rice

1982–86 Menil Collection, Houston

1988–94 Kansai International Airport, Osaka, Japan

1989 Awarded the RIBA (Royal Institute of British Architects) Gold Medal

1991–98 New buildings, Potsdamer Platz, Berlin (Potsdamer Platz arcades, Casino)

1991–98 Jean-Marie Tjibaou Cultural Centre (Nouméa, New Caledonia, southwest Pacific)

1992–97 Fondation Beyeler, Riehen, Switzerland

1993 Founds the Renzo Piano Building Workshop

1994–2002 Parco della Musica Auditorium, Rome

1998 Awarded the Pritzker Prize

1999–2005 Paul Klee Centre, Riehen, Bern, Switzerland

2000–07 New York Times Building, New York

Architecture and surroundings in close union: Jean-Marie Tjibaou Cultural Centre in Nouméa

Kansai International Airport, Osaka

1868 Shogun Tokugawa Yoshinobu surrenders

1886 Statue of Liberty, New York

1883 First petrol-driven automobile, Gottlieb Daimler and Carl Benz

1914–1918 First World war

1929 Start of the Great Depress

1931 Wakatsuki jiro resign Prime Min of Japan

1840–1895 REVIVALISM   **1895–1910 ART NOUVEAU**   **MODERNISM 1910–1980**

| 1850 | 1855 | 1860 | 1865 | 1870 | 1875 | 1880 | 1885 | 1890 | 1895 | 1900 | 1905 | 1910 | 1915 | 1920 | 1925 | 1930 | 1935 |

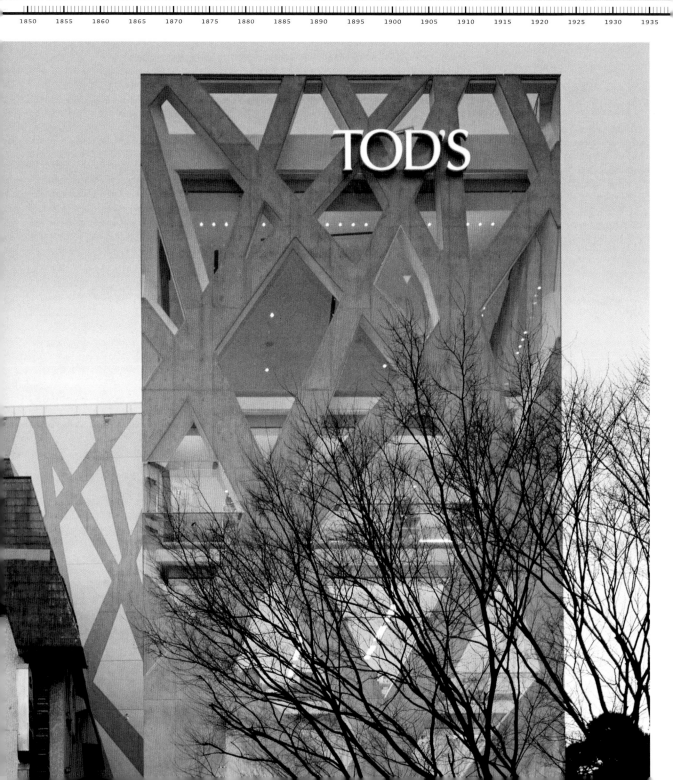

7 Guernica, Pablo Picasso   1948 Assassination of Mahatma Gandhi
1939–1945 Second World War   1949 Birth of the People's Republic of China   1973 First oil crisis
1941 Japanese attack on Pearl Harbor   1961 Berlin Wall erected
1945 Atomic bombings of   1965 Nobel Prize (Peace) for United Nation's Children's Fund (UNICEF)
Hiroshima and Nagasaki
1990 German reunification
2001 September 11 attacks
1910–1980 MODERNISM   POST-MODERNISM FROM 1980

TADAO ANDO, JAPANESE ARCHITECT

1940   1945   1950   1955   1960   1965   1970   1975   1980   1985   1990   1995   2000   2005   2010   2015   2020   2025

TOYO ITO

"Architecture must adapt to the diversity of society, and must reflect the fact that a simple square or cube cannot contain this diversity." It would indeed be fruitless to search for a simple square or cube in the buildings of Toyo Ito.

The curious, imaginative forms that Toyo Ito gives his buildings show the extent to which this architect has internalized this concept. For a long time it has been his declared goal to hold flowing and floating forms, *ephemeres*, fast in his architecture. The present, and the dynamics of big-city life, challenge Ito to responses in the form of buildings.

In 1976, in order to create a secluded space away from the bustle of Tokyo, Ito built for his sister and her two daughters a private house, White U, right in the center of the city. The building lies in a U-shape around a grassed inner courtyard, to which the roof gently slopes down. Light enters the inner courtyard through skylights and windows. Right next to it, several years later, Ito built his own house, which bears the poetic name Silver Hut. This hut, however, does not lie in a wood, but because of its location represents a unit largely closed off from the outside world. This one-story building consists of a roof construction of silvery reflecting steel barrel vaults, supported by reinforced concrete pillars. Above the inner courtyard is placed a removable tent roof. Thus, according to requirements, this unusual complex can be given an additional space. Interior and exterior, tradition and innovation merge naturally into each other.

One of Toyo Ito's most striking works is the Tower of Winds. Purely architecturally, this is a conversion around an exhaust air system, but visually it is an interactive installation, which reacts to the light, sound and wind of its environment (Tokyo inner city) with its own light and sound signals. Thanks to aluminum and acrylic mirror panels, a computer-driven spectacle of colors and sounds can be experienced at night. The neon rings placed around the tower make the structure very light and almost ephemeral, further underlining the changing impulses. An "Egg of Winds" was later created in a Tokyo car park: at night a gigantic aluminum egg is transformed into an artistic projection surface for images from five different sources.

As early as 1986, with his interactive tower, Ito made the interplay of technology, man, and architecture his constant theme. His preoccupation with this question was based on the nomadic status of big-city dwellers, for whom Ito developed flexible architectural units and some utopian projects. The apparently short-term nature of some of Ito's works could also be derived from Japanese architecture: thus, in comparison to Europe, there is little urban planning, and the threat of earthquakes in the area has traditionally made the house into something short-lived. The poetic momentum of his forms and the lightness of his construction certainly originate from this attitude. His preferred materials, apart from concrete, are aluminum and every kind of perforated, punched metals, which particularly as elements of his façades give his buildings a kind of weightlessness.

1941 Born 1 June, in Seoul, Korea
1965 Receives his diploma in architecture from the University of Tokyo
1965–69 Works with Kiyonari Kikutake, a co-founder of the Metabolists
1971 Founds his firm URBOT (short for Urban Robot)
1976 White U, private house, Tokyo
1979 Renames his firm to Toyo Ito and Associates, Architects
1984 Silver Hut, his own residence
1986 Tower of Winds
1995–2001 Sendai Mediatheque
2002 Summer pavilion of the Serpentine Gallery, London
2002–04 Tod's Omotesando store, Tokyo
2006 Tod's Omotesando store, Tokyo
2006 Matsumoto Performing Arts Centre, Nagano
2006 Awarded the RIBA (Royal Institute of British Architects) Gold Medal
2006–09 Opera House, Taichung, Taiwan

left page
Ito's building for Tod's echoes the theme of the widely branching Zelkova trees that edge the street

left
The residential project White U, built for Ito's sister

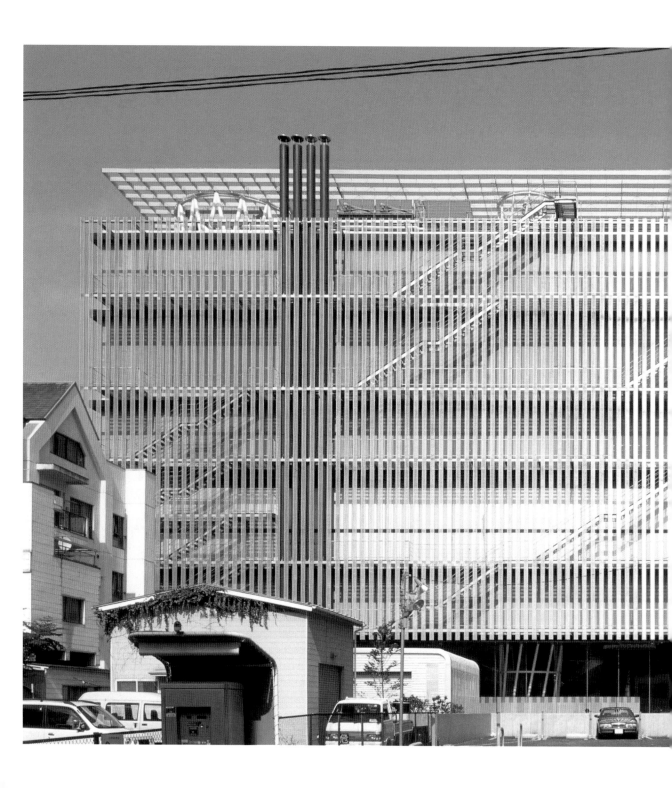

Up to the present day, Ito has retained the ambition to do justice to the new challenges of city and environment, and offer new architectural solutions. His buildings, accordingly, are conceptually designed, and he often describes them in metaphorical terms. "To talk about architecture and explain it is difficult, for architecture inevitably has two sides. On the one hand it is an abstract model of ideas, and on the other something that exists in reality."

In the Mediatheque at Sendai there are no longer any traditional library spaces; all intervening walls are omitted in favor of an open space that is given rhythm by apparently arbitrarily grouped columns. It is Ito's declared aim to bring the physical and the virtual world into harmony in his buildings, and thus to create in his architecture spaces for our contemporary needs. Each of us, according to Ito, has a real and a virtual body, an originally human one and one that has come into being through the extension of our everyday life by the media. His architecture is intended to take account of both bodies. In the same way, the life of the real city and the virtual cosmos are linked together.

This ambition is reflected in the flowing, organic forms of the Opera House in Taichung, Taiwan. The intention is that the spaces should be adapted to the art of singing from East and West. Instead of steel supports and walls, the building seems to consist of curved membranes. The architect calls his project "Sound Cave." The acoustic space is in reality a whole network of cave-shaped spaces, which also communicate with the surroundings.

In the 21st-century city, everything depends on movement, sound and images—and Toyo Ito is creating the buildings for them.

Open space, divided only by columns: the Mediathèque of Sendai

1868 Shogun Tokugawa Yoshinobu
surrenders

1883 First petrol-driven automobile,
Gottlieb Daimler and Carl Benz

1886 Statue of Liberty, New York

1914–1918 First World war

1929 Start of the
Great Depres

1931 Wakatsu
jiro resig
Prime Mi
of Japan

1840–1895 REVIVALISM   1895–1910 ART NOUVEAU   MODERNISM 1910–1980

| 1850 | 1855 | 1860 | 1865 | 1870 | 1875 | 1880 | 1885 | 1890 | 1895 | 1900 | 1905 | 1910 | 1915 | 1920 | 1925 | 1930 | 1935 |

Transcendent design element as part of the
architecture: the Church of Light

Guernica, Pablo Picasso   **1948** Assassination of Mahatma Gandhi   **1965** Nobel Prize (Peace) for   **1990** German reunification
1939–1945 Second World War   **1949** Birth of the People's Republic of China   United Nation's Children's
1941 Japanese attack on Pearl Harbor   **1961** Berlin Wall erected   Fund (UNICEF)   **2001** September 11 attacks
1945 Atomic bombings of Hiroshima and Nagasaki

1910–1980 MODERNISM   POST-MODERNISM FROM 1980

1940   1945   1950   1955   1960   1965   1970   1975   1980   1985   1990   1995   2000   2005   2010   2015   2020   2025

TADAO ANDO

Ando's architecture was once compared with the Japanese tea ceremony: "Both are enclosed and concentrated. Both have a deliberately created simple appearance. Both are calm, quiet, pure. Both are gentle, austere and clear in mood. Both are dimly lit but have light within their darkness. Both give a feeling of expansiveness in spite of their small size. Though set in cities, both are rural in nature. Though artificial, both are natural."

This description is wonderfully accurate about the buildings created since 1969 by the former professional boxer and self-taught architect Tadao Ando. His spaces, composed of clean materials, always giving an impression of nobility, and are such that visitor can, indeed must, react physically to them. The architect himself explains this with reference to the special Japanese sense of physicality, and the way in which the body reacts to specific spaces. It is such considerations that determine his approach to design. Formed from geometric elements, his minimalist designs are characterized by other pure materials such as steel, glass, wood, and his hallmark silky concrete.

The sensual (extra-sensory) element of Ando's work is visible particularly in his Church of Light in Ibariki, where the most important symbol of the Christian religion, the cross, is formed by slits in the walls through which sunlight enters a relatively dark inner space, creating a positively mystical atmosphere. It is the presence and the perception of the human being that makes the interplay of nature (sunlight) and the deliberately simple geometry into a functioning whole.

In 1992 Tadao Ando built the Japanese pavilion for the World's Fair in Seville. This consisted of a gigantic wooden building with an inward-curving façade, which was accessible by way of an arched staircase, and had a flat Teflon roof. The building resonates with clear references to Japanese architectural and craft traditions, and is at the same time very modern.

One of Ando's most impressive projects is the island of Naoshima. There he has created a center of nature and art, to which new buildings have regularly been added for more than 15 years. For example, a guesthouse and various exhibition spaces have already been built on the island, which is distant from the bustle of the city and can be reached only by boat. Here, in the middle of nature, partly resembling a natural resource, lie concrete structures in geometric forms, whose interior spaces surround the exhibited works of art with a special atmosphere. The Chichu Museum of Art (*chichu* means underground) is a concrete building for the most part buried in the earth, with an unusual interplay of landscape, natural light, and interior space. Lucid geometry and a highly sophisticated use of daylight give an attractive Zen atmosphere to these rooms, built to display the art of Claude Monet, Walter de Maria, and James Turrell.

In Germany, Ando has built the Langen Foundation on the Hombroich Missile Base at Neuss, which, much like the buildings on Naoshima, stands in an interesting relationship to its natural environment, with a large pool of water, earthworks, and cherry trees. Although glass walls allow a view of the outside, the exhibition rooms appear as though detached from the outside world, and form a cosmos all of their own, in which one can come closer to art. Ando creates spaces for the dialogue between man, art, and nature.

His architecture, according to a book title, is an architecture of silence, and this is not inaccurate: there are no noisy effects, no crashing forms, no raging demands for applause—but the positive echo is everywhere.

1941 Born 13 September, in Osaka, Japan
1951–58 Studies model building in wood with a carpenter
1962–69 Travels through Europe, USA, Africa. Becomes fascinated with architecture
1969 Founds the Tadao Ando Architect & Associates in Osaka
FROM 1987 Teaches in the USA and Japan
1987–89 Church of Light, Ibariki, Osaka
1992 Japanese pavilion at the World's Fair in Seville
FROM 1992 Buildings on Naoshima
1995 Awarded the Pritzker Prize
1997 Awarded the RIBA (Royal Institute of British Architects) Gold Medal
2001 Pulitzer Foundation for the Arts, St. Louis
2004 Chichu Art Museum, Naoshima

1871 Foundation of the German Empire

1872 * Piet Mondrian,
Dutch painter, born

1890 Dutch painter Vincent van Gogh dies

1866 * Wassily Kandinsky,
Russian painter, born

1914–1918 First World war

1929 Start of the
Great
Depression

1840–1895 REVIVALISM   1895–1910 ART NOUVEAU   MODERNISM 1910–1980

| 1850 | 1855 | 1860 | 1865 | 1870 | 1875 | 1880 | 1885 | 1890 | 1895 | 1900 | 1905 | 1910 | 1915 | 1920 | 1925 | 1930 | 1935 |

The Casa da Música in Porto was built as
part of Porto's project for European
Culture Capital in 2001 (completed in
2005)

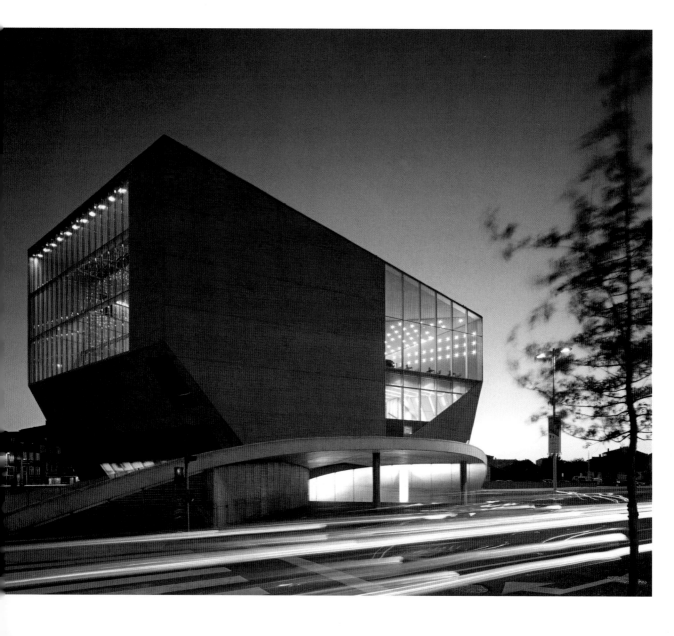

1939–1945 Second World War   1961 Berlin Wall erected   1969 Neil Armstrong is the first person to set foot on the Moon   ZAHA HADID, IRAQI-BRITISH ARCHITECT
        1944 Allied troops land on the beaches   1963 John F. Kennedy   1972 Summer Olympics take place in Munich
            of Normandy during D-Day   assassination in Dallas, Texas
        1949 Democratic Republic of Germany 1964 Dutch architect and designer Gerrit Rietveld dies   1990 German reunification
            DDR established officially   2001 September 11 attacks

                    1910–1980 MODERNISM   POST-MODERNISM FROM 1980

1940   1945   1950   1955   1960   1965   1970   1975   1980   1985   1990   1995   2000   2005   2010   2015   2020   2025

REM KOOLHAAS

As a thinker, author, and architect, the Dutch architect Rem Koolhaas has had a great impact on contemporary architecture. Even before he attracted international attention with his buildings, he was giving food for thought to his colleagues with his books and other writings.

In *Delirious New York, a Retroactive Manifesto for Manhattan* (1978) he confronted the uncontrollable growth of cities in the age of globalization. His 1,376-page *S,M,L,XL* (1995) on the other hand gives an overview of Koolhaas' entire work up to that point, and on the other examines the connections between architecture and modern society. Incidentally, this book, whose layout, reminiscent of collages and video clips, was developed by Kohlhaas in co-opera-tion with the Canadian graphic artist Bruce Mau, and altered the structure of architectural books worldwide.

This Dutch "prophet of a new modern architecture" was born in 1944 in Rotterdam, where today the headquarters of his Office for Metropolitan Architec-ture (OMA) is located. But he was no stay-at-home. Between 1952 and 1956 he lived with his parents in Indonesia, an experience that has proved a lasting influence on him. He began his professional career as a journalist and screenwriter, before turning to architecture and studying from 1968 to 1973 at the Architectural Association in London and Cornell University in New York. Up to 1979 he was Visiting Fellow and the Institute for Architecture and Urban Studies in New York, which was directed by the Deconstructivist Peter Eisenman. Together with Elia and Zoe Zenghelis and Madelon Vriesendorp, in 1975 he founded OMA in London; in 1980 it was moved to Rotterdam.

Architecture and Cities

During the first years there were only a few building commissions, but these created a sensation: the Netherlands Dance Theater in The Hague (1987) and the Kunsthal in Rotterdam (1992). Unexpected spa-tial programs, crooked levels, new forms, suspended gravity—all the limits of the conventional were crossed. Finally, the concrete house in Bordeaux (1998) which, with a workspace that also serves as a lift, was designed for a wheelchair user, brought him international success. With this house alone, in the

judgment of the jury for the Pritzker Prize, which was awarded to Koolhaas in 2000, its creator would go down in architectural history.

The buildings that followed, always realizations of his theory of merging "bigness," technology, and progress with humanity, are no less trend-setting, such as his Netherlands Embassy in Berlin (2003), Seattle Central Library (2004), and the Casa da Musica in Porto (2005). To be able to continue working on his many conceptual projects beyond architecture and urban planning, in 2002 he founded the "think tank" AMO. OMA*AMO is today directed by six partners, has more than 230 staff from 30 different countries, and runs further offices in New York and Beijing. His order book is full. Hamburg, Qatar, Dubai, Beijing, and New York will see OMA buildings that would have been unimaginable only a few years ago.

1944 Born 17 November, in Rotterdam, Holland
1952–56 Lives in Jakarta, Indonesia, and from 1956 in Amsterdam
1960s Works as a screenwriter and as a journalist
1968–72 Studies at the Architectural Association School of Architec-ture (AA) in London
1972–73 Studies at Cornell University, New York
1973–79 Teaches in the USA and Holland
1975 Founds Office for Metropolitan Architecture with Zoe and Elia Zenghelis and Madelon Vriesendorp
1978 Publishes *Delirious New York, A Retroactive Manifesto for Manhattan*
1980 Founds OMA in Rotterdam
1988–89 Teaches at the Technical University of Delft
FROM 1990 Teaches at Harvard University
1991–92 Teaches at Rice University, Houston, Texas
1995 Publishes *S,M,L,XL*
2000 Awarded the Pritzker Prize
2002 Founds AMO
2004 Awarded the RIBA (Royal Insti-tute of British Architects) Gold Medal

Despite its three dwelling levels, Koolhaas' house in Bordeaux is attuned to the requirements of the wheelchair-using client

The CCTV Headquarters in Bejing will have 51 floors

1887–1889 Construction of the Eiffel Tower in Paris

1914–1918 First World war

1929 Start of the Great Depression

1852 Napoleon III becomes Emperor of the French

1870–1871 Franco-Prussian War

1890 * Charles de Gaulle, French general and statesman, born

1919 Treaty of Versailles

1926 French painter Claude Monet dies

1840–1895 REVIVALISM   **1895–1910 ART NOUVEAU**   **MODERNISM 1910–1980**

| 1850 | 1855 | 1860 | 1865 | 1870 | 1875 | 1880 | 1885 | 1890 | 1895 | 1900 | 1905 | 1910 | 1915 | 1920 | 1925 | 1930 | 1935 |

Award-winner: the Institut du Monde Arabe in Paris

JACQUES HERZOG UND PIERRE DE MEURON, SWISS ARCHITECTS   1990 German reunification

1939–1945 Second World War   1961 Berlin Wall erected   1981 François Mitterrand   1991 The Warsaw Pact is officially dissolved

1949 The Federal Republic of   1968 Student riots in Paris   becomes French President

Germany is established   1986 Chernobyl nuclear reactor disaster   2001 September 11 attacks

1910–1980 MODERNISM   POST-MODERNISM FROM 1980

1940   1945   1950   1955   1960   1965   1970   1975   1980   1985   1990   1995   2000   2005   2010   2015   2020   2025

JEAN NOUVEL

Architecture students have much to learn from Jean Nouvel: how to deal with materials, light and shade, transparency and the illusion of de-materialization, the integration of a building into the site in question and its history, richness of metaphors, the unexpectedly new and different, the playful and the serious, elegance and the grand gesture—all expressed in built architecture.

Architecture students have much to learn from Jean Nouvel: how to deal with material, light and shade, transparency and the illusion of de-materialization, the integration into the site in question and its history, richness of metaphors, the unexpectedly new and different, the playful and the serious, elegance and the grand gesture—all expressed in built architecture.

Grands Projets

Nouvel's first building to attract attention, which most expertly incorporates all the qualities named above, is the Institut du Monde Arabe, with which he achieved his international breakthrough. It was one of the *grands projets* of François Mitterrand, who helped Paris to achieve new splendour in the 1980s with symbolic major projects. The Institut du Monde Arabe received the Equerre d'Argent for the best French building in the year of its completion, 1987. There followed one masterpiece after another, such as the rebuilding of the Lyon opera house, whose new glass barrel roof merges with the 19th-century substructure into a harmonious "total work of art" (for this too, Nouvel received an Equerre d'Argent in 1993); the main body of the Fondation Cartier in Paris, apparently dematerialized between two reflecting glass walls; the Galeries Lafayette store of 1995 in Berlin; and, in 2000, the Cultural and Congress Center in Lucerne, which with its strongly protruding roof makes an unprecedented architectural statement and at the same time reflects the lake and the surrounding mountain world. The Torre Agbar, the new landmark of Barcelona (2005), towers up from the ocean of houses like a monolith, its colors constantly changing, while the Musée du Quai Branly in Paris, opened in 2006 and dedicated to the art of Africa, Oceania and Asia, with its apparently arbitrary juxtaposition of the most diverse structures, speaks a whole new architectural language again.

Political Past and Architectural Future

Born in 1945 in the small village of Fumel in south-west France, Jean Nouvel at first wanted to study painting, but then signed up for architecture and in 1970, while still a student, founded his first architectural office. Brought up in the political climate of the 1960s, he also became committed to the social role and political responsibility of architecture. In 1976 be became a co-founder of the architectural movement Mars, and a year later of the Syndicat de l'architecture, which is still active today. In 1978 he founded the Architectural Biennale in the context of the Paris Biennale.

The Ateliers Jean Nouvel today employ more than 150 staff from 25 countries, where not only architects, but also urban planners, landscape architects, model builders, graphic artists working in the media, industrial designers, and interior designers work together. Jean Nouvel Design reflects the master's enthusiasm for product design. In the Ateliers, work is in progress on more than 40 projects to be realized worldwide in the next few years.

1945 Born 12 August, in Fumel, Lot-et-Garonne, France

1966–72 Accepted as best applicant at the École Nationale Supérieure des Beaux-Arts in Paris; 1972, gains hid diploma in architecture

1967–70 Assistant to Claude Parent and Paul Virilio

1970–72 Founds his first office with François Seigneur

1972–81 Architectural co-operative with François Seigneur and Gilbert Lézènes

1976 Co-founds the architectural movement Mars 1976

1977 Co-founds the Syndicat de l'Architecture

1978 Founds the Architectural Biennale in the context Paris Biennale

1981–84 Works with Gilbert Lézènes and Pierre Soria

1984–1989 Founds the office of Jean Nouvel et Associés

1989–1994 Founds the office Jean Nouvel et Emmanuel Cattani

1993 Receives the Equerre d'Argent prize for the Opera House, Lyon

1994 Founds the Ateliers Jean Nouvel

1995 Becomes an honorary member of the Royal Institute of British Architects, London

2000 Golden Lion of the Venice Biennale

2006 International Highrise Award for the Torre Agbar, Barcelona

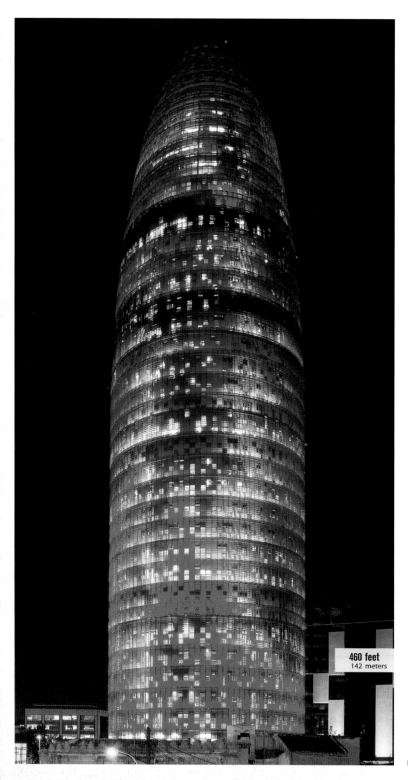

460 feet
142 meters

Play of colours – the Torre Agbar in Barcelona

1891 End of the Indian Wars in the USA

1886 Statue of Liberty, New York

1883 First petrol-driven automobile,
Gottlieb Daimler and Carl Benz

1928 * Andy Warhol,
American artist, bor

1914–1918 First World war

1929 Start of the
Great
Depression

1840–1895 REVIVALISM   **1895–1910 ART NOUVEAU**   **MODERNISM 1910–1980**

| 1850 | 1855 | 1860 | 1865 | 1870 | 1875 | 1880 | 1885 | 1890 | 1895 | 1900 | 1905 | 1910 | 1915 | 1920 | 1925 | 1930 | 1935 |

Libeskind's extension to the Denver Art
Museum, completed in 2006

7 *Guernica*, Pablo Picasso   **1950** India becomes a republic   **1963** John F. Kennedy assassination in Dallas, Texas

1939–1945 Second World War

1948 United Nations General Assembly adopts
Universal Declaration of Human Rights

1967 Six-Day War in the Middle East

1986 Chernobyl nuclear
reactor disaster

1990 German reunification

2001 September 11 attacks

2003 Third Gulf War (US invasion of Iraq)

1910–1980 MODERNISM   POST-MODERNISM FROM 1980

1940   1945   1950   1955   1960   1965   1970   1975   1980   1985   1990   1995   2000   2005   2010   2015   2020   2025

DANIEL LIBESKIND

His first building hit the German architectural landscape like a bolt of lightning. Usually the beginning of an architect's career is marked by smaller commissions such as single-family houses. Daniel Libeskind's first work, however, was the complex Jewish Museum in Berlin, which made him world-famous at a stroke.

Architecture As Language

Not, of course, on account of the sheer size of the museum, but because of its unusual structure and power of expression. The metaphor of lightning is apt here not only in a figurative sense; it is also at the basis of the ground plan, which Libeskind has significantly conceived as a distorted Star of David. So-called "voids," empty spaces extending over five floors in the interior of the building, symbolize the absence of the Jewish population of Berlin. Slanting window slits cut like knife-slashes into the outer skin of the building.

These examples already demonstrate Libeskind's understanding of architecture: for him architecture is a language—full of metaphors, allusions, and historical references to the place for which it is intended. His plans and sketches are scattered with explanations and addenda. Philosophy, literature, history, music: all disciplines flow into his Deconstructivist designs, which brings him on the one hand an enthusiastic band of followers and on the other the criticism that his architecture is overloaded with meaning.

This intellectual, always black-clad, gentle and friendly outsider was born 1946, the son of Jewish Holocaust survivors, in Lodz, Poland. His family emigrated to Israel in 1957 and settled in the USA in 1960. In 1965 Libeskind became an American citizen. Before turning to architecture, he studied music in Israel and at first practiced as a professional musician. In 1965–1970 he studied at the Cooper Union School of Architecture, New York, and in 1970–1971 studied architectural history and theory as a postgraduate student at the University of Essex in England. There followed years of teaching at various English universities and in the United States. For the building of the Jewish Museum, he moved to Berlin with his family in 1989. He attracted further attention with various follow-up commissions such as the Danish Jewish Museum in Copenhagen, the spectacular Imperial War Museum in

Manchester and a private gallery in Majorca. He was heaped with awards and honorary doctorates. But what finally catapulted him into public attention worldwide was the first prize in the 2002 competition for the Ground Zero master plan in New York.

Ground Zero

With this remarkable design, Libeskind remained true to his principle of *architecture parlante*. The buildings' names alone speak volumes—Memory Foundations, Freedom Tower—as do the symbolism of numbers (the Freedom Tower was to be 1,776 feet high, a reference to the year of the American Declaration of Independence) and the formal and visual references to the Statue of Liberty. But real life spoke a different language. The site owners and developers found the design too extravagant and too expensive. What remained of the dream of the Freedom Tower was merely the height of 1,776 feet (541.3 meters), after another firm, SOM (see page 149), had been entrusted with executing the plans. Of the overall plan, only the Memory Foundations remain on the project list of Studio Daniel Libeskind (SDL), which moved to New York in 2003 and employs 70 staff there. But in the wake of the Ground Zero debate, SDL is booming. Further branches of the firm have opened in Zurich, Milan, San Francisco, Denver, Toronto and wherever new Libeskind buildings are being created; orders have come in since then from all over the world.

1946 Born 12 May, in Lodz, Poland
1957 Emigrates with his family to Israel, and studies music there
1960 Moves to the USA
1965–70 Becomes an American citizen, and starts a course of study in architecture at the Cooper Union of the Advancement of Science and Art, New York
1971/72 Postgraduate study of architectural theory and history at the School of Comparative Studies, Essex, England
1978–85 Becomes the Dean of the Department of Architecture, Cranbrook Academy of Art, Bloomfield Hills, Michigan
FROM 1985 Teaches in England and the USA, from 1999 in Germany, then worldwide
1986–1989 Becomes the founder and director of Architecture Intermundium, Milan
1989 Wins 1st prize in the competition for the Jewish Museum in Berlin, and establishes an office in Berlin
1997 Awarded an honorary doctorate by the Humboldt University, Berlin
1999 Awarded German Architectural Prize for the Jewish Museum in Berlin
2003 Awarded 1st prize in the competition for the rebuilding of the World Trade enter, New York.
2007 Receives the Großes Verdienstkreuz from the Federal Republic of Germany

1883 First petrol-driven automobile,
Gottlieb Daimler and Carl Benz

1886 Statue of Liberty, New York

1891 End of the Indian Wars in the USA

1914–1918 First World war

1928 * Andy Warhol,
American artist
born

1929 Start of the
Great
Depression

1840–1895 REVIVALISM   1895–1910 ART NOUVEAU   MODERNISM 1910–1980

| 1850 | 1855 | 1860 | 1865 | 1870 | 1875 | 1880 | 1885 | 1890 | 1895 | 1900 | 1905 | 1910 | 1915 | 1920 | 1925 | 1930 | 1935 |

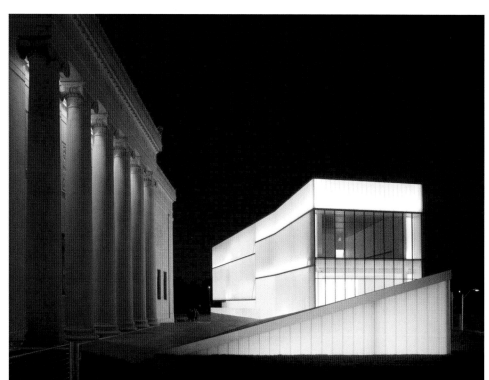

Stone and feather: Holl's Bloch Building
for the Nelson-Atkins Museum of Art in
Kansas City

DANIEL LIBESKIND, AMERICAN ARCHITECT

7 *Guernica*, Pablo Picasso   **1950** India becomes a republic   **1959** Frank Lloyd Wright's Guggen-
   1939–1945 Second World War   heim Museum is completed
       1948 United Nations General   **1963** Assassination of John F. Kennedy
          Assembly adopts Universal   **1967** Six-Day War in the Middle East
          Declaration of Human Rights   **1910–1980 MODERNISM   POST-MODERNISM FROM 1980**

1990 German reunification **2001** September 11 attacks
                 1997 Frank O. Gehry's Guggenheim
1986 Chernobyl nuclear   Museum Bilbao is completed
     reactor disaster   **2003** Third Gulf War (US invasion of Iraq)
           1993 The Maastricht Treaty takes effect, formally
                 establishing the European Union

1940   1945   1950   1955   1960   1965   1970   1975   1980   1985   1990   1995   2000   2005   2010   2015   2020   2025

STEVEN HOLL

"Seven bottles of light in a stone box"—on this image is based one of Steven Holl's best-known buildings, the chapel of St Ignatius on the campus of Seattle University. This concept refers to the various light situations in the different sections of space in the building, arranged according to liturgical symbolism, which are created by colored windows in the interior.

The forms filled with light by Steven Holl are of the most varied shapes. What is common to his buildings as a special feature, however, is his use of natural or artificial light, and its skilful continuation into the interior of the architectural structure.

On completing his studies in Washington and Rome in 1976, Steven Holl opened an office in New York, which remains today the base for his activities. A further office has been added in Beijing. At the beginning of his career he published the magazine *Pamphlet Architecture*, and his preoccupation with architectural theory has continued for almost 30 years in his work as a professor at Columbia University in New York.

His creative approach to his designs is often conceptual and driven by philosophical considerations. Often he sums up his concept in a few words noted on his artistic sketches. For Holl, inspiration is always closely connected with the prospective site of the intended building.

In the case of the Bloch Building of the Nelson-Atkins Museum of Art in Kansas City, Missouri, opened in 2007, it could have been the inscription of the façade of the existing museum from the 1930s, with its imposing columned frontage, that led him to his concept: "The soul has greater need of the ideal than of the real."

Here, on the basis of the opposing pair, stone and feather, Steven Holl developed a series of formal demands on the extension building for which he had been commissioned. The great majority of the new exhibition spaces are located underground. As complementary contrasts to the old museum and its surrounding park, five irregularly formed building structures are visible above ground level, which are linked together underground. The lenses (as the architect calls the upper parts of the extension building) are composed entirely of special frosted glass. This matches the color of the sky by day, and conveys the light to illuminate the dynamically designed interior spaces. At night, the glass boxes,

now appearing to be floating, are lit up and form surrealistic-looking sources of light for the park and the sculpture garden.

Steven Holl was able to realize a variant of this play with light at the Faculty of Philosophy of the University of New York: here it is a question of an interior rebuilding, whose concept is derived from Holl's interest in phenomenology and the theories of Ludwig Wittgenstein. Unusual reflections of light are created in the newly designed stairwell—as an inspiration for the students who pass through?

Steven Holl's biggest project at present is a city within a city, an impressive residential development in Beijing. The project is called Linked Hybrid on account of its multifarious uses, with residential areas, shops, leisure centers and offices. Eight asymmetrically positioned towers are linked together by bridges. As with many of Holl's projects, great value is placed on ecology. The complex is geothermally air-conditioned. One comment stated that the complex was like a 21st-century version of the Forbidden City. Holl's city, however, will be very accessible.

1947 Born 9 December, in Bremerton, Washington
1970 After graduating from the University of Washington, studies in Rome
1976 Joins the Architectural Association in London and founds his own office in New York
FROM 1981 Teaches at Columbia University, New York
1994–97 Chapel of St Ignatius, Seattle University
1999–2002 Simmons Hall students' residence, Massachusetts Institute of Technology, Cambridge
1992–98 Kiasma Museum for Contemporary Art, Helsinki
1997–2005 Pratt Institute, Brooklyn, Higgings Hall extension
1999–2007 Nasher-Atkins Museum of Art, Kansas City
2001–05 Luisium Hotel, Langenlois, Austria
2003–08 Linked Hybrid, residential complex, Beijing
2004–07 New York University, rebuilding of Faculty of Philosophy

The future of architecture: Holl's design for Linked Hybrid, a "city within the city" in Beijing. As well as 750 apartments, plans for the complex include a hotel, a kindergarten, shops and car parks

1886 Statue of Liberty, New York

1928 *Andy Warhol, American artis born

1883 First petrol-driven automobile, Gottlieb Daimler and Carl Benz

1914–1918 First World war

1929 Start of the Great Depression

1840–1895 REVIVALISM   **1895–1910 ART NOUVEAU**   **MODERNISM 1910–1980**

1850   1855   1860   1865   1870   1875   1880   1885   1890   1895   1900   1905   1910   1915   1920   1925   1930   1935

Dynamic: the Phaeno Science Center – the experimental landscape in Wolfsburg

REM KOOLHAAS, DUTCH ARCHITECT

Guernica, Pablo Picasso

1939–1945 Second **1948** United Nations General
World War Assembly adopts Universal
Declaration of Human Rights

1963 John F. Kennedy assassination in Dallas, Texas

1979 Saddam Hussein becomes Iraqi President
1979 Ruhollah Khomeini seizes power in Iran

1980–1988 Iran-Iraq War
(First Gulf War)

1986 Chernobyl nuclear
reactor disaster

2001 September 11 attacks

1990 German reunification
1990–1991 Second Gulf War

2006 Saddam Hussein dies
2003 Third Gulf War (US invasion of Iraq)

1910–1980 MODERNISM   POST-MODERNISM FROM 1980

1940   1945   1950   1955   1960   1965   1970   1975   1980   1985   1990   1995   2000   2005   2010   2015   2020   2025

ZAHA HADID

If her brothers had had their way, she would have become the first female Iraqi astronaut. Now Zaha Hadid is the first woman to have received a Pritzker Prize (in 2004) and to be among the world stars of architecture. That should satisfy even the most ambitious of brothers.

But success came only after years of consistent hard work—and until a client had the courage to translate Hadid's architectural visions into reality. For however much her abstract drawings were admired and her competition designs were honored with prizes, they were ahead of their time and were considered as simply impractical.

Single-minded belief in progress had been Zaha Hadid's heritage from birth. The mood in Iraq at the time was marked by optimism. Born in Baghdad in 1950, she received an excellent education, made possible by her parents, and crowned between 1972 and 1977 by a course of study at the Architectural Association in London. Her teachers, Rem Koolhaas (see page 153) and Elia Zenghelis, of whose Office for Metropolitan Architecture she was a member between 1978 and 1980, were ideal patrons and encouraged her in the further development of her spatial concepts.

Influenced by Russian Constructivism and on the lookout for new presentation media beyond simple engineering drawings, Hadid first adopted painting as a medium of expression. In order to depict adequately our complex, postmodern age with its ever changing dynamics and new social structures, spatiality had to be newly defined: space itself was distorted and displaced, layered and overlaid, so that a new space continuum could be created. Hadid's early sketches look as though they had been drawn on a computer, long before such programs came on the market.

Architecture for the New Millennium

In 1980 Hadid founded her own architectural office in London. During the following decade, however, her desk was heaped not with building commissions, but with teaching appointments. The lecture halls of the most renowned architectural schools were full to bursting when she spoke on her concepts. She won competitions. Her design for the restaurant on the Hong Kong Peak of 1983 has become iconic, at least since 1988 when it was exhibited in the celebrated Deconstructivism exhibition at the Museum of Modern Art in New York. But it has never been built.

The first of Hadid's structures in real concrete, steel and glass came into being in 1993, with the fire station of the Vitra furniture company at Weil am Rhein: a little architectural sensation. Her next competition designs, including the Cardiff Bay Opera House (first prize in 1994), again remained unrealized. It was only the elegant Bergisel ski-jump in Innsbruck (2002) and the Rosenthal Center for Contemporary Art in Cincinnati, Ohio, (2003) that finally brought the breakthrough. Since then, cultural centers, industrial headquarters, and sports facilities have emanated, and are still emanating worldwide, from the laboratory of this energetic woman. Her architecture is probably best suited to the 21st century.

1950 Born 31 October, in Baghdad, Iraq
1972–77 Studies at the Architectural Association School of Architecture in London
1977 Awarded the Diploma Prize of the Architectural Association
1977–87 Teaches at the Architectural Association
1978–80 Works as a partner in the Office for Metropolitan Architecture with Rem Koolhaas and Elia Zenghelis, London
1980 Founds her own office
1987, 1993 AND 1998–1999 Teaches as a visiting professor of architecture at Columbia University, New York
1988 Takes part in the exhibition *Deconstructivist Architecture* at MoMA, New York
1994 Awarded first prize in the competition for the Cardiff Bay Opera House, Cardiff, Wales (not realized)
2004 Awarded the Pritzker Prize
2006 Retrospective at the Guggenheim Museum, New York
2007 Exhibition at the Design Museum, London

Enthusiasts for architecture are drawn to Weil am Rhein: here Hadid built the headquarters of the Vitra Fire Station (now closed down)

Flowing forms in the midst of a
mountain world: the Hungerburg
railway in Innsbruck

LE CORBUSIER, SWISS ARCHITECT

ALBERTO GIACOMETTI, SWISS PAINTER AND SCULPTOR

1871 Foundation of the German Empire

1872 *Impression, Sunrise*, Claude Monet

1866 * Wassily Kandinsky, Russian painter, born

1881 * Pablo Picasso, Spanish artist, born

1911 * Max Frisch, Swiss architect and poet, born

1914–1918 First World war

1929 Start of the Great Depression

1840–1895 REVIVALISM   1895–1910 ART NOUVEAU   MODERNISM 1910–1980

| 1850 | 1855 | 1860 | 1865 | 1870 | 1875 | 1880 | 1885 | 1890 | 1895 | 1900 | 1905 | 1910 | 1915 | 1920 | 1925 | 1930 | 1935 |

Former power station as museum: the Tate Modern Gallery in London

1939–1945 Second World War
1944 Allied troops land on the beaches of Normandy during D-Day
1946 First meeting of the United Nations

1961 Berlin Wall erected
1972 Summer Olympics take place in Munich
1963 John F. Kennedy assassination in Dallas, Texas
1969 Neil Armstrong is the first person to set foot on the Moon

2001 September 11 attacks
1990 German reunification

1910–1980 MODERNISM POST-MODERNISM FROM 1980

1940 1945 1950 1955 1960 1965 1970 1975 1980 1985 1990 1995 2000 2005 2010 2015 2020 2025

HERZOG & DE MEURON

None of their buildings is like any other. The designs from the studio of the two Swiss architects Jacques Herzog and Pierre de Meuron are all of the very highest quality—each individual building is a tailor-made one-off.

Haute Couture Architecture

But name labels and instructions for care are not part of the package: a building must have a direct impact and speak for itself.

The characteristic quality of their architecture lies not in a recognizable, repeating vocabulary of forms, but on another level. It is its constant ability to surprise and amaze, its innovative use of materials and new developments in construction technique. It is its impressive quality of design, its Swiss precision, and at the same time its total artistic freedom; not only do the buildings have the effect of works of art, but many also come into being in close cooperation with artists such as Rémy Zaugg, Thomas Ruff, Rosemarie Trockel, Michael Craig-Martin, and Ai Weiwei. That the function of a building cannot be read from its outer form is another trait of the architecture of Herzog and de Meuron. At the same time, however, all their buildings are outstandingly appropriate to their purpose, whether they are art galleries, sports stadiums, or administrative buildings. And they are clearly conceived solely for the place where they stand. Not only the topography, but also the constraints and needs of the location are seen by Herzog and de Meuron as a challenge and an opportunity to find new constructive and aesthetic solutions. However much their most recent works oppose our visual habits, they arouse thoroughly positive emotions. More than this, they creep into the hearts of their users, often even before they are completed, and become the trademark of a firm, the symbol of a city, the pride of a nation.

From Lego House to Bird's Nest

The architectural duo have for a long time been supported by a further seven partners and more than 250 staff, distributed worldwide in offices in Barcelona, Peking, Munich, London, and San Francisco. But the headquarters of the firm is in Basel, where both Jacques Herzog and Pierre de Meuron

were born (on 19 April and 8 May 1950 respectively). What is remarkable is that the two have not only worked together since they both studied architecture at the Federal Institute of Technology (ETH) in Zurich (1970–1975), but have actually been friends since their childhood days, even if their sandcastles and Lego houses of those days did not yet hint at their later career, and both came to architecture only by a roundabout route. After completing their studies, both continued for three years as assistants at ETH, and in 1978 they founded their own office in Basel, which grew slowly but steadily in importance. Apart from building commissions, they also accepted teaching appointments: at Harvard University (from 1993) and at the ETH in Zurich (from 1999) up to the present day. Although they were already long known beyond the borders of Switzerland, their rebuilding of a former power station in London as a museum space for the Tate Modern gallery in 2000 brought them their international breakthrough. And it was undoubtedly their brilliant rededication of a gigantic industrial building that led to the Pritzker Prize in 2001, and to worldwide major commissions such as the extension to the Walker Art Center in Minneapolis (2005), the Allianz football arena in Munich (2005), the Hamburg Elbphilharmonie concert hall (2008), and the Olympic stadium in Beijing (2008). The stadium, known as the "Bird's Nest" on account of its outer skin of steel "twigs," was hailed by *Time* magazine as early as a year before its completion as one of ten architectural masterpieces of 2007.

1950 Jacques Herzog and Pierre de Meuron born in Basel, Switzerland
1970–75 They study architecture at the Federal Institute of Technology (ETH), Zurich
1975–78 Work as assistants at ETH
1978 Found a joint architectural practice in Basel
FROM 1993 Teach as visiting professors at Harvard University
FROM 1999 Teach as professors at ETH Zurich
2001 Awarded the Pritzker Prize
2002 Found the ETH Studio, Basel
2003 Awarded the RIBA (Royal Institute of British Architects) Stirling Prize
2004–06 *Herzog & de Meuron. No. 250. An Exhibition*, Basel, Munich, Rotterdam, etc.
2007 Awarded the RIBA (Royal Institute of British Architects) Gold Medal
2007 Praemium Imperiale of the Japan Art Association

A bird's nest for sporting records: the
Olympic Stadium in Beijing

PHOTO CREDITS

Alexander Langkals, Landshut: Frontispiece
Nigel Young/Foster + Partners: pp. 10/11, 118, 119
Foto Scala, Florence: pp. 18, 21
Herbert Hartmann, Munich: p. 14
Achim Bednorz, Cologne: pp. 15 bottom, 16, 30
Bilderberg, Hamburg: pp. 22, 46
Giovanni Simeone: pp. 24/25
James L. Stanfield/Getty Images: pp. 28/29
Florian Monheim: p. 32
ARTUR: Cover (Farnsworth House, Louvre), pp. 34, 67 left, 72, 80, 86/87, 90, 100, 116, 136, 137, 142, 150, 160/161
LOOK: pp. 36, 48, 92, 93
Jürgen Hohmuth, Berlin: pp. 38/39
akg-images: pp. 41, 53 right, 55, 65, 71 right; David Borland: p. 83; Florence Delva: p. 61 bottom; Hedda Eid: p. 129 left; Electa: p. 133; Hilbich: pp. 50; Erich Lessing: pp. 40, 54 left; Bruni Mea: p. 115; Jürgen Raible: pp. 51, 54 right; Gert Schütz: p. 77
Postsparkasse Wien Bibliothek: p. 44
Sabine Thiel-Siling: p. 59 top right
Michael Freeman: pp. 58/59
Paul Rocheleau Canaan, Richmond: p. 56
LAIF: Cover (Stadium Beijing), p. 60
Archives nationales/Institut francais d'architecture, Fonds Perret: p. 61 top
Werner Neumeister: p. 62
Ezra Stoller/Esto: pp. 66, 96, 102
Hans Engels: pp. 68/69
Hervé Champollion: p. 70
Frank den Oudsten: p. 74
Mario Carrieri for Cassina: p. 75 bottom
Tim Street-Porter/Esto: p. 76
Photos courtesy Dion Neutra, Architect and Richrad J. Neutra Papers, Department of special Collections, Charles E. Young Research Library, UCLA, Fotografer Julius Shulman, Los Angeles, Callifornia: pp. 78/79
Eino Mäkinen, Alvar Aalto Museum: p. 82
Kazi Khaleed Ashraf: p. 84
Getty Images: Cover (Florence), pp. 12 top, 89

Norman McGrath: p. 88
Eckhard Ribbeck: p. 91
Osamu Murai: p. 98
John Nye, Hong Kong: p. 103
Rainer Kiedrowski: p. 104
Behnisch Architekten: p. 105 top
Buchheim Museum, Bernried: p. 105 bottom
Bildagentur Huber, Garmisch-Partenkirchen, Picture Finders: p. 106
Todd Eberle: pp. 109, 163
John Sullivan: p. 111
Burg/Schuh BFF, Palladium Fotodesign, Cologne, Berlin: p. 112
IFA Bilderteam, Munich, Siebig: p. 114
Ian Lambot, Hong Kong: p. 119 left
Andrew Ward: p. 119 right
Marcus Bredt: p. 122
Heiner Leiska: p. 123
Skidmore, Owings & Merril: pp. 124, 126, 127
Lluís Casals: p. 128
John Gollings: p. 130
Gianni Berengo Gardin: p. 131
RPBW Shunji Ishida: p. 132 top
Shinkenchiku-sha: p. 132 bottom
NACASA & Partners, courtesy of TOD's: p. 134
Mitsuo Matsuoka: p. 138
Tadao Ando Architects and Associates: pp. 140/141
OMA: p. 143 bottom
Iwan Baan: pp. 144/145, 164/165
Gaston: p. 146 top
Georges Fessy: p. 146 bottom
Philippe Ruault, Nantes: pp. 148, 149
Studio Daniel Libeskind: pp. 151–153
Andy Ryan: p. 154
Courtesy Mark Heithoff: p. 155
Steven Holl Architects: pp. 156, 157
Werner Huthmacher: p. 158
Steve Double: p. 159 top
Christian Richters, Münster: p. 159 bottom

INDEX

Aalto, Alvar 80
Alberti, Leon Battista 14
Ando, Tadao 138

Behnisch, Günter 104
Bernini, Gianlorenzo 26
Bramante, Donato 16
Brunelleschi, Filippo 12
Burnham, Daniel 46

Foster, Norman 118

Gaudí, Antoni 48
Gehry, Frank O. 108
Gerkan, Meinhard von 122
Gropius, Walter 62

Hadid, Zaha 158
Herzog, Jacques 162
Holl, Steven 154
Horta, Victor 54

Ito, Toyo 134

Jefferson, Thomas 36
Johnson, Philip 88

Kahn, Louis I. 84
Koolhaas, Rem 142

Le Corbusier 70
Ledoux, Nicolas 34
Libeskind, Daniel 150

Marg, Volkwin 122
Meier, Richard 116
Meuron, Pierre de 162
Michelangelo 18
Mies van der Rohe, Ludwig 66
Moneo, Rafael 128

Neumann, Balthasar 32
Neutra, Richard 76
Niemeyer, Oscar 90
Nouvel, Jean 146

Palladio, Andrea 22
Pelli, Cesar 106
Pei, Ieoh Ming 100
Perret, Auguste 60
Piano, Renzo 130

Rietveld, Gerrit 74
Rogers, Richard 114
Rossi, Aldo 112

Saarinen, Eero 94
Schinkel, Karl Friedrich 38
Semper, Gottfried 42
SOM 124
Sullivan, Louis 52

Tange, Kenzo 96

Wagner, Otto 44
Wren, Christopher 30
Wright, Frank Lloyd 56

TEXTS

Isabel Kuhl: pp. 12, 14, 16, 18, 22, 26, 30, 32, 34, 36, 38, 42, 44, 46, 48,
    52, 54, 56, 60, 62, 66, 70, 74, 76, 80, 84
Kristina Lowis: pp. 88, 90, 94, 96, 100, 106, 112, 114, 116, 118, 122, 124,
    128, 130, 134, 138, 154
Sabine Thiel-Siling: pp. 108, 142, 146, 150, 158, 162